What every Canadian
should know
about

FAMILY
FINANCE

**CANADIAN
SECURITIES
INSTITUTE**

Montreal • Toronto • Calgary • Vancouver

Credits
Managing Editor: Dominic Jones
Writer: Chuck Midgette
Design & Illustrations: Bowness & Yolleck Communications Inc.
Copy Editors: Catherine Shearer-Kudel & Paul Irwin

Canadian Cataloguing in Publication Data

Main entry under title:
What every Canadian should know about family finance
ISBN 1-894289-07-2
1. Finance, Personal – Canada.   I. Canadian Securities Institute
HG179.F36 1999   332.024'00971   C98-932911-9
First Printing 1999 by the Canadian Securities Institute
Copyright 1999 © the Canadian Securities Institute

CANADIAN SECURITIES INSTITUTE

121 King Street West, Suite 1550,
Toronto, Ontario M5H 3T9
Tel: 416-364-9130 Fax: 416-359-0486

Printed and bound in Canada by Key Interactive Inc. a Dollco Communications Co.

Making sense of investing

Now it's easier for you to become a better investor! This average-level book is suitable if you already know the basics but want to expand your knowledge to a semi-professional level.

Investor Learning Centre
OF CANADA

The Investor Learning Centre of Canada (ILC) is an independent not-for-profit organization dedicated to providing independent investment information to Canadians. It was established in 1996 by the Canadian Securities Institute, the national educator for the securities industry.

The ILC offers books, seminars, resource centres and Internet services across Canada.

Introduction

C hances are you already know quite a bit about financial planning. Your understanding of the subject may have started with your childhood allowance, and the realization that 20 or 30 foregone candy bars could get you a baseball glove or a Barbie doll. Today, while the expenditures are many times larger, you continue to make the same rough calculations when it comes to allocating your resources between clothing, food, transportation, shelter and, lest we forget, having a bit of fun along the way.

Like the grasshopper in Aesop's fable, you may even be familiar with the concept of setting aside part of your current harvest for the future. Maybe you contribute to an RRSP. Maybe you realize how many thousands of dollars in interest you can save by paying off your mortgage early. Maybe you have even delved into investments such as mutual funds or stocks and bonds. The fact is, most Canadians do these things in one form or another. It's equally true, however, that only 15% of us do so according to an overall financial plan that puts a real price tag on our future needs and lays out a specific strategy to meet them. That's a real tragedy, one this book is designed to help you avoid.

The uncertain road ahead

In recent generations, the consequences of such complacency weren't quite as severe. In the early 1950s, for example, most Canadians quit work at age 65 and looked forward, on average, to four years of retirement. RRSPs didn't exist, but most retirees fared pretty well on a combination of government and employer-provided pensions, plus whatever personal savings they had managed to accumulate along the way.

How quickly times have changed. Today, the average 65-year-old can look forward to 13 years in retirement. While that's certainly a welcome development, the gradual aging of the population is diminishing our ability to fund what we once considered sacrosanct social programs. In 1951, Canada had a relatively young population with seven people of working (and tax-paying) age for each retiree. In 1995, that ratio was about five to one. By 2030, the ratio is expected to drop to three to one. That will put a severe strain on social programs like the Canada Pension Plan, which has never been funded to meet its future obligations. Governments will be hard pressed to raise taxes any further on the dwindled base of increasingly burdened taxpayers. As a result, Canadians likely will be expected to take a much larger role in funding their own retirement. The federal government has already set the stage for this new reality with generous tax breaks for RRSPs. Unfortunately, many Canadians don't take advantage of them regularly.

Similar budgetary pressures have made financial planning necessary in other aspects of life. More and more families are looking after aging parents, sometimes while they fund their children's education. Meanwhile, government cut-backs are making both obligations more expensive all the time.

Ratio of retirees to working-age Canadians

1951	1995	2030
Working-age Canadians to retirees 7:1	Working-age Canadians to retirees 5:1	Working-age Canadians to retirees 3:1

Source: The Canadian Global Almanac/Canadian Institute of Actuaries

Fewer working-age Canadians to each retiree will put severe strain on social programs. The only safety net we can rely on might very well be the one we finance ourselves.

Since the early 1980s at least, there's been an added phenomenon. Large numbers of people with solid work experience have found themselves thrown out of work. Employers use the terms "downsizing" or "rightsizing." Some firms just go bankrupt, while a number of others happen to be subsidiaries of foreign-owned companies that prefer to minimize the job losses in their native countries. The affected employees — many in their 50s and early 60s, and from white- and blue-collar positions — have a difficult if not impossible time of finding new employment. The truly lucky ones — those given a generous golden parachute — can go into business for themselves, ride out their unemployment or, if their means allow, end their working lives early. Not that many people, though, are so fortunate.

Under these circumstances, many families are having trouble making ends meet, let alone setting

3

aside part of their income for tomorrow. Higher taxes and stagnant incomes have reduced real income in recent years and impaired the ability of many Canadians to save. The savings rate is at its lowest level in more than two decades, while the ratio of household debt to disposable income is higher than ever.

Financial plight of the Canadian family

Heavily taxed, the average Canadian family has little left after basic expenses. We spend more on taxes than on shelter. And we're spending more for government services like health care and education, while cutting back on food and clothing. Remember that for many of the expenses in the chart below, there's at least a piece that goes to the government through additional taxes like GST and sin taxes.

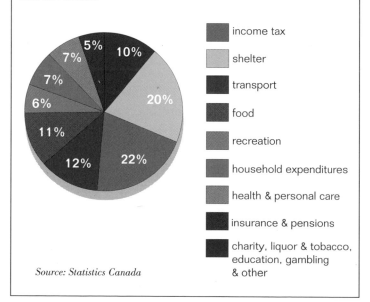

- income tax
- shelter
- transport
- food
- recreation
- household expenditures
- health & personal care
- insurance & pensions
- charity, liquor & tobacco, education, gambling & other

Source: Statistics Canada

There's yet another challenge facing families today. With 15- to 24-year-olds experiencing the highest level of unemployment of any age group — Statistics Canada figures reveal that from the mid- to late 1990s, the unemployment rate for this group was nearly double that of 25- to 65-year-olds — many adults are having to house or otherwise help their children much longer than expected. Whether it's higher grocery and utility bills, loans to their kids or other expenses, these families are having to tighten their belts even further, or draw upon savings normally earmarked for retirement.

You can change your future

Fortunately, you can take control of the future. And the good news is that it doesn't require winning the lottery or getting a hefty raise tomorrow morning to do it. The biggest reason most Canadians fail to achieve financial security and independence isn't a lack of income, it's a lack of planning.

That's not to say that financial planning is an easy process. It takes a lot of hard work and sacrifice. But people with a plan are better able to keep on plugging because they have a strong sense of where their journey is leading and how long it will take to reach their destination. Of course, the direction and pace of our individual journeys will be unique, depending on many different circumstances including career, income, marital status and number of children. Like fingerprints, each financial plan is different. If you are like most other Canadians, however, your plan will

5

probably include most of the following goals:

- establishing a safety net;
- buying a home;
- saving for a comfortable retirement;
- paying off the mortgage; and,
- saving for your children's education.

No matter where you want to go in life, a well-conceived financial plan is the single best thing you can do to make sure you get there. It's the only way to ensure that you carefully consider and articulate your goals, put a price tag on achieving them, and set aside a predetermined amount each year to make them come true. This book will help you start your journey.

Where are you financially?

The cornerstone of sound family finance is knowing where you are, where you want to be, and mapping a strategy to get there.

To start, calculate your net worth

To chart a course for the future, it's important to know where you want to go. But it's equally important to determine how far away you are from your destination. To do that, you have to get a fix on your current position. When it comes to financial planning, your current position is known as your *net worth*.

Over time, your net worth statement will provide a reliable snapshot of your financial health and allow you to adjust your financial plan to make sure you arrive at your destination on schedule.

Net worth:
The total market value of all owned assets, such as your home and investments, minus what you owe on your mortgage, credit cards and loans.

For an individual or family, a net worth statement is the basic measure of financial health. Simply defined, it's the total fair market value of all assets owned, such as a house, savings or investments, minus the total value of all outstanding liabilities like mortgages and other loans. In other words, net worth is the amount by which your assets exceed your liabilities at any time. The net worth statement represents a snapshot in time of your financial assets and it will grow over time to fund future spending needs.

The process of preparing a financial plan and the initial calculation of net worth begins with pulling together all the relevant financial records. These include your latest tax returns, bank statements, canceled cheques, credit card information, monthly statements for all household expenses, RRSP and mutual fund records, mortgage statements, loan information, insurance records and pension statements.

Coming up with all this information may seem like a daunting task, but it's an essential first step in taking control of your financial future. Not only do these records provide the information you need to calculate your net worth, they lay the foundation for risk management, savings, credit, debt, investment, tax, retirement and estate planning.

The worksheet on the next page has most of the basic elements you need to get started. If you have assets or liabilities that aren't listed here, simply add them in the spaces provided.

Check your net worth annually

The net worth figure is important because it forms the basis of all your subsequent calculations. Remember, though, it's just a snapshot, while wise financial planning is a motion picture. Your net worth at the end of a given year, or any other anniversary of the specific date you first measure it, should be compared on a regular basis to your figure from the previous year. Only in that way can you determine if the current rate of growth in your net worth is sufficient to reach your goals. You may not always like what you see, but by measuring your progress on at least an annual basis, you'll be able to determine if your current savings and investment strategies are meeting your long-term financial targets. If they are, the annual calculation of net worth will provide valuable peace of mind. If they aren't, you'll gain the earliest possible signal to revise your wealth-building strategies.

Financial planning: *The process of ensuring all aspects of your financial situation are properly organized and directed to achieving your goals.*

9

Calculating Your Net Worth

ASSETS	You	Spouse	Total
Possessions			
house			
car(s)			
furniture			
cottage			
antiques			
artwork			
collectibles			
other			
Savings and Investments			
savings/chequing accounts			
treasury bills			
Canada Savings Bonds			
GICs and other term deposits			
stocks			
bonds			
RESPs			
mutual funds			
cash value of life insurance			
real estate			
other investments			

Retirement Savings	You	Spouse	Total
RRSPs			
pension plans			
deferred profit sharing plans			
Total Assets			
LIABILITIES			
Personal Debts			
mortgage(s) on home			
other mortgages			
car loan(s)			
line of credit			
credit card balances			
other loans			
unpaid bills			
outstanding taxes			
other			
Total Liabilities			
NET WORTH	You	Spouse	Total
Assets			
(minus) Liabilities			
Equals: YOUR NET WORTH			

Measure your cash flow

Once you've determined your net worth, you'll know your present position. But an equally important first step in the journey to financial peace of mind is figuring out where your money is coming from and how you're spending it. While the secret of financial planning may seem very complicated, it's really quite simple: you have to spend less than you earn. Making sure you do that starts with what's called *cash management planning*.

Getting started is a relatively simple process with the aid of a cash flow management statement, as presented on pages 12 and 13. If you already maintain a regular budget, filling out this statement should be simple. If you don't, a quick review of your chequebook, credit card invoices, savings account statements and regular bills can provide an accurate record of monthly receipts and expenditures. From there, it's a fairly simple matter of annualizing your income and expenses, although you might need a few months of figures to accurately estimate certain expenses, such as water or heating, that may vary a lot from season to season.

*Cash management planning:
The process of determining all the sources of household income and expenses during the year.*

After completing this exercise, most people discover they have a positive cash flow. But it's too early to congratulate yourself.

Financial planners generally estimate that the average Canadian family needs to save about 20% of gross annual income to realize their financial goals. For most Canadians, those goals include owning a home, funding their children's education and providing for a comfortable and interesting retirement. However, the 20% figure is just an estimate. The amount of savings you require will depend on many individual factors including your current net worth and your personal financial targets.

What Canadian families spend their money on

Personal income taxes	$10,630
Shelter	$9,870
Transport	$6,200
Food	$5,700
Clothing, health & personal care	$3,730
Household expenditures	$3,620
Personal insurance & pension contributions	$2,780
Recreation	$4,780
Cash, gifts & charity	$1,240
Liquor & tobacco	$1,140
Miscellaneous	$800
Education	$660
Reading materials	$280
Gambling	$250

Source: Statistics Canada

Cash Flow Statement

Income
All Sources of Income

salaries	$_____	
self-employment	$_____	
dividends/interest	$_____	
capital gains	$_____	
rents/annuities/pension	$_____	
bonus/gifts/misc. income	$_____	
alimony/child support	$_____	
other	$_____	
TOTAL INCOME	$_____	_____%

Expenses
Taxes & Deductions

federal	$_____	
provincial	$_____	
CPP/UIC	$_____	
Total Taxes & Deductions	$_____	_____%

Home

mortgage or rent	$_____	
insurance	$_____	
utilities, phone, tv	$_____	
tax	$_____	
Total Home	$_____	_____%

Basic Needs

food	$_____	
clothing	$_____	
healthcare	$_____	
Total Basic Needs	$_____	_____%

Insurance Premiums

life, disability, health	$_____	
auto	$_____	
Total Insurance Premiums	$_____	_____%

Other Debts

Car Instalment/Leases $_____

charge accounts $_____

other $_____

Total Other Debts $_____   _____%

Flexible Family Needs

vacations $_____

entertainment $_____

tuition $_____

other $_____

Total Flexible Family Needs $_____   _____%

Appliances & Expenditures

major appliances $_____

major expenditures $_____

other $_____

**Total Appliances &
Expenditures** $_____   _____%

Miscellaneous

charity $_____

other $_____

alimony/child support $_____

Total Miscellaneous $_____   _____%

Savings

registered savings $_____

non-registered savings $_____

other $_____

Total Savings $_____   _____%

TOTAL EXPENSES $_____   _____%

**Total Income
minus** $_____

**Total Expenses
equals** $_____

Total Cash Flow $_____

Planning to save

Financial security requires setting realistic goals, creating a sound strategy to achieve them and, of course, action.

Set priorities for your family

As in every other aspect of life, setting goals is an essential part of the planning process. As the old Chinese proverb warns: "If you don't know where you are going, any old road will do." If you expect to turn your dreams into reality, you and the rest of the family have to take the time to establish specific goals. Even the best-laid plans, of course, are subject to change. But this shouldn't prevent you from getting started. Your financial plan is a living document and it can always be altered to suit your changing objectives.

If you find that the cost of all your dreams far exceeds your ability to pay for them, welcome to the club. We live in a world of unfulfilled desires. Consumers are saturated with clever advertising designed to make them feel a painful gulf between the way they are and the way they could be if only for want of something new or better. Sometimes, it's difficult to resist the consumerist pull, especially when the increasing availability of credit makes the process seem so painless.

Identify needs vs. desires

The key is to be able to recognize the difference between wants and needs. You might want to buy a luxury sports sedan instead of a minivan. You might want to take the family on a cruise rather than spend a week camping at a provincial park. Who wouldn't? But many people choose not to exercise these options — even when they are affordable — because the financial planning process forces you to recognize the difference between desires and needs. It forces you to make important choices.

It also makes you realize that the decisions you make early in life will have a profound effect on your financial security and freedom when you're much older. That's not to say that choosing a luxury vacation instead of making your maximum RRSP contribution means that you'll be eating canned spaghetti in retirement. The consequences of our decisions are a lot more difficult to sort out than that. But the fact is, financial security and the freedom to make choices later in life depend on recognizing that every decision is not an isolated event. The choices you make now will affect the choices you are able to make later. And the only way to put a price tag on each of these decisions, of course, is to start with a financial plan.

*RRSP:
Registered
Retirement
Savings Plan —
gives you a tax
deduction and
lets your
investments
grow tax free
until age 69.*

Strategies to help you save

Once you have identified your goals, the next step is finding a way to pay for them. No doubt your salary will probably increase in the years ahead, but chances are, you and the government will quickly find ways to spend it. The best approach always is to find more creative ways to save more of what you earn now. And the best way to do that is to consider savings to be a fixed expense — a bill you must pay every month — just like your mortgage or utility bills.

Of course, most of us fail to look at savings this way. The result is that we usually live up to our means, often going in debt whenever we need to replace the furnace or buy a new car. A much better approach is to treat savings as a fixed expense and not the varying amount of spare change that's lying around after all other needs have been met.

Another technique you can use to accelerate your journey to better financial health is to treat any raise, bonus, inheritance or windfall as added money to invest. This may not always be possible, but try to resist the temptation of splurging on a deluxe vacation, or however else you might be tempted to spend the money.

The savings that you'll need to increase your net worth can be generated in one of three ways: an increase in assets, a decrease in liabilities, or a combination of both. Here are a few proven strategies to help you get started.

Set easy initial goals
Unrealistic goal setting is perhaps the most common reason people give up on financial planning. In their zeal to drive home the seriousness of saving for the future, many financial experts suggest that a savings goal of about 20% of gross income is necessary for most people. But if your family is already having trouble making ends meet, a high target is bound to fail. The best rule is to start small. Set an initial savings goal that the family believes can be met with a bit of effort. Over time, you will get used to the idea of setting aside something for future needs and you can increase your contribution as circumstances permit.

Start an automatic savings plan
One of the most painless ways to save money is to make sure you never have an opportunity to spend it. For example, many employees take advantage of automatic

payroll deduction plans to invest in Canada Savings
Bonds. Those who lack access to payroll deduction
might choose to set up preauthorized chequing for the
purchase of mutual funds. The strategy here is simple.
Treat this money as if you never even received it. Most
often, you'll find a way to get along without it. In the
meantime, you'll watch your investments grow
impressively over time.

Pay cash or don't spend
Canadians are giving into the temptation of credit like
never before. In 1997, for example, Canadians put
some $16.5 billion in purchases on credit. By
comparison, the figure was only $7.9 billion in 1988.
Yet by making it a habit to pay cash for most of the
things you buy, you can save a lot of money. Not only
will you save on interest charges, you will also earn
interest on your money while you save for your
purchase. The benefits are especially big if you rely on
credit cards too much and don't pay your balance every
month. We'll have more to say on that subject in the
next chapter.

However, if you are a very disciplined person and
never carry a balance, you might find credit cards a
handy way to keep track of how you spend your money.
The monthly statement you receive can give you a
bird's-eye view of your purchases over time. And, if
your card allows you to rack up frequent flyer or
merchandise points, you may be able to spend less on
vacations or household items.

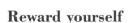

Reward yourself

Saving for retirement or educating your children is a long and difficult undertaking. Sometimes, living mainly for tomorrow might not seem worth the effort. That's why many families make a point of rewarding themselves with some fun along the way. For example, you might decide to treat yourself to a short vacation if you've met your annual long-term savings goals.

Cut your expenses

When it comes to finding the extra money you need to meet your financial goals, the first order of business is to carefully analyse expenses. Pay particular attention to flexible items that can be trimmed without adversely affecting your lifestyle. These generally include personal things such as clothing, grooming, dining out and entertainment, but can also include big-ticket items such as home remodeling and vacations.

One of the most practical

8 Practical Tips to Help You Save

If you...

1. Drive to work...

2. Want to buy a new car, but your current one still runs well...

3. Need to repair or remodel your home...

4. Love to see the latest movie as soon as it has been released...

5. Love to stock your bookcases with the latest titles...

6. Contract a company to cut the grass or shovel snow...

7. Eat out often because you get home late or are too tired to cook...

8. Enjoy exercising but don't want to pay hefty fitness club fees...

Consider...

Taking public transit, at least part of the time.
A monthly transit pass could be far less than parking
fees alone.

Hanging on to it for another year or so. The
difference between loan payments and repairs
is money you could invest.

Taking a good look at what you can do yourself and
what should be left to tradespeople. Having a
plumber unclog the kitchen sink could easily cost
you $75, while buying or renting a tool to do the job
yourself likely will cost far less.

Catch a matinee, go on a Tuesday evening when
the admission is reduced, or wait until it comes out
on video. If you have young kids, video rentals will
save a bundle on babysitting and theatre snacks.

Wait a little while and borrow books cost-free from
your public library.

Hiring a reliable teenager to do the work.

Buying prepared foods such as fresh pasta and
sauce from a deli or grocery.

Investing in a couple of workout tapes or a piece of
equipment like a stationary bike or cross-country
ski machine. In the first year alone you could be
further ahead financially.

cost-reduction strategies is to track all known monthly expenses and make reasonable estimates for the year. If some categories strike you as high — you might be surprised to learn that spending about $7 for a modest lunch every day at work costs almost $1,700 a year — then you'll be in a better position to make adjustments to certain spending habits. By going through this exercise with all spending, you'll have the foundation of a budget that will help you find the money you need to save regularly. After reading the list of suggestions on the previous page, chances are you have a number of ideas to add from your own experience.

Chapter 3

Credit and debt planning

**While credit isn't inherently evil,
you should know how it works and when to use it.**

Everyone needs credit

While it would be nice to go through life without ever paying a cent in interest, the fact is, it's just not an option for anyone but the independently wealthy. Most of us simply aren't able buy a $160,000 home with what's stashed in the bank. That's why mortgages — with payback or amortization periods of up to 25 years — are a fact of life. Indeed, for most people, buying a car or meeting unexpected expenses such as a leaky roof or a new furnace requires a little help from the bank. In such cases, credit is a convenient way to overcome the temporary imbalance between earnings and expenditures.

Compound interest: When your money seems to grow magically because you're getting interest on interest you've already earned.

The key word here, however, is *temporary*. As we've said, the problem with credit is that far too many people rely on it and live beyond their means indefinitely.

Use credit cards with care

One of the easiest ways to fall into debt is with credit cards. And why not? More convenient than cash, they provide free money for up to a month as long as you make the minimum monthly payment. For those people who do, it almost seems as if the banks are running a charity.

Fortunately for the banks, many people don't pay off their balances in full every month. Many plan to, but somehow they get into the habit of buying a few more items than their income will cover each month. While modest at first, the balance usually starts to snowball quickly. One of the reasons for this is that you begin to pay interest on the interest. At around 18% for a bank credit card, your balance can start to grow pretty fast. What's worse, the bank is concerned not by the size of your debt, but your ability to carry it. That's why the higher your outstanding balance, the higher the credit limit you are granted, provided you are willing and able to make the minimum monthly payment.

Retail credit cards

Department stores and other retailers also offer

What credit really costs

If you used your credit card to buy a pair of tickets to a musical or big sports event for $150 and didn't pay for them until three months later, you'd pay $156.75, including interest at 18% per year. If you took a full year, those tickets would cost you $177 — almost $30 or 20% more than their original price. Imagine how much more expensive a big-ticket item like a fridge would be if you took several months to pay for it!

credit cards. There was a time when these retailers wouldn't accept Visa or MasterCard, because they didn't want to pay the card issuer a percentage of each transaction, especially when they had their own credit cards to promote. In the end, convenience to the consumer prevailed and bank credit cards are now accepted by most major retailers, including the department stores that continue to offer their own cards. For most people, carrying a retail credit card makes no sense unless you're receiving important membership benefits and are religiously paying your account in full every month. Failure to do so is costly, since the annual rate of interest on many department store credit cards is almost 30%.

It's also a good idea to have as few cards as possible from banks, retailers or both. Not only will this curb the temptation to buy, you'll have fewer monthly statements to keep track of. And with fewer bills arriving each month, it's easier to ensure you pay your bills in full and on time.

Shop around for personal loans

Most personal loans are granted for a specific purpose such as buying a new car or consolidating all your other debts into a single loan. For instance, it's quite common for people to pay off unwieldy credit card balances by taking out a personal loan, which typically carries about half the rate of interest of the debt it replaces. Regardless of the purpose, a schedule of monthly payments is then set up to retire the loan. Usually, you can choose from a variety of payment options including a fixed or variable rate of interest.

Consolidate debt: *Use a lower interest loan to pay off higher interest debts to reduce overall interest costs.*

As we've said, paying interest on borrowed money isn't the best way to achieve financial security. However, if you do have to borrow, it pays to shop around. The banks and other financial institutions are in competition to invest the money in their savings accounts, and rates will vary from one bank to another depending on the amount of surplus cash they want to put to work. Lenders will also have some flexibility in the rate they can offer you, especially when spreads between prevailing interest rates and the rate of inflation are relatively high.

Personal lines of credit for emergencies

Many people set up a line of credit with their financial institution to cover unexpected costs. Much like a personal chequing account that's been stocked with the bank's money, a *line of credit* lets you write cheques for whatever purpose you deem worthy up to the limit in the account — usually $10,000 to $50,000 depending on your creditworthiness. Compared to credit cards, personal lines of credit are relatively inexpensive. A *secured line of credit* (one where you've pledged assets as collateral for the loan) charges about *prime* plus 1% for outstanding balances. Unsecured lines typically charge prime plus 4%.

The line of credit can also be a relatively cost-effective way of setting up an emergency fund for your family. In past years, most financial planners recommended setting aside two to six months' salary before saving for a house or making other investments. But it takes a long time to save that kind of money, and such delays are costly in terms of foregone investment earnings. Relying on a line of credit as your emergency fund may allow you to put your money to better use.

Line of credit: *A special banking priviledge that lets customers write cheques up to a certain total amount, often between $10,000 and $50,000.*

Secured line of credit: *The customer pledges personal assets such as a home as security.*

Prime: *The interest rate banks charge their best customers.*

How much credit can you handle?

Unfortunately, too many Canadians can't answer this question until their loan applications are rejected. Decisions to grant credit for personal loans, home mortgages, credit cards or other purposes are made according to common criteria that describe your overall capacity for credit. These include the total debt service ratio and gross debt service ratio.

Total debt service ratio

One rough guide to how much debt you can comfortably handle is the *total debt service ratio*, or in the language of bankers, TDS. It's defined as your monthly rent or mortgage payments, plus property taxes, plus debt payments, divided by your monthly gross family income. For example, if you have a mortgage of $1,000 a month, property taxes of $300 per month, a monthly car loan payment of $300, and a gross family income of $4,600 per month, your total debt ratio would be:

Total debt service ratio:
The sum of your monthly mortgage payments and property taxes, or rent, plus loan payments, divided by your monthly gross family income. The ratio is expressed as a percentage.

Gross debt service ratio:
A simpler formula which excludes loans.

$$\frac{\$1,000 + \$300 + \$300}{\$4,600} \quad x \quad 100 = \mathbf{35\%}$$

Generally speaking, financial institutions are happy to open up the purse strings if your TDS is less than 40%. In this case, you would have the capacity to take on more debt.

Gross debt service ratio

The other rough guide financial institutions use to measure your debt capacity is the *gross debt service ratio* or GDS. Similar to the TDS, but a little bit easier to calculate, it's simply monthly mortgage or rent payments plus property taxes divided by gross monthly income. Using the same assumptions, your GDS would be:

$$\frac{\$1,000 + \$300}{\$4,600} \quad x \quad 100 \quad = \quad \mathbf{28\%}$$

Ideally, financial institutions prefer to see a GDS no higher than 30%.

If you have a good credit rating — that is, a track record of paying your bills on time — and your TDS and GDS ratings indicate you can handle more debt, most financial institutions would be happy to extend credit. Remember, though, that each situation is different and that just because you qualify for credit doesn't mean you should take advantage of it. And if you have large child care, medical or other expenses, carefully consider what additional credit you can handle before you sign a loan or credit application.

Managing your biggest debt: the mortgage

You can save thousands by making the right mortgage choices.

The real value of your home

Owning a house is an almost universal dream of Canadians. But it's also an expensive one. In Canada, the average price of a home is about $155,000 and it may be significantly higher in major cities like Vancouver and Toronto. Most first-time buyers, of course, don't have that kind of money lying around and must rely on financial institutions for loans that are many times larger than their annual income. In the process, they take on a mountain of debt that will end up costing two or three times as much as the value of the mortgage itself. Given this reality, why would anyone in their right mind consider buying a home?

Benefits of owning your own place
The simple answer is that, despite their enormous financing cost, the benefits of owning a home generally outweigh the costs. Let's start with the emotional benefits. For most of us, the four walls around us are a home, the physical foundation of family life. It's an oasis, a refuge and an expression of our personalities. No wonder people grow so attached to them.

Traditionally, houses have also been a solid investment and one of the cornerstones of a sound financial plan. Over a recent 18-year period, real estate has kept well ahead of inflation with an average annual increase in value of 7.6%. Even when performance isn't very robust, real estate is still regarded as a sound investment. Why? Because land is a limited commodity and the population of the country continues to increase.

Average home resale prices in Canada versus inflation

Home resale prices in Canada showed a steady increase almost every year from 1980 to 1998, while inflation took a bit of a roller coaster ride. On average, residential real estate during this time climbed 7.5% per year, while inflation rose by an annual average of only 4%. In other words, resale prices kept well ahead of inflation.

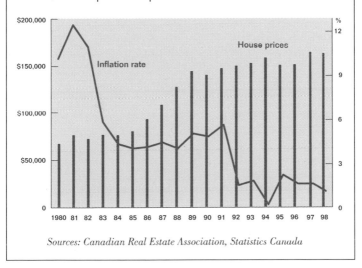

Sources: Canadian Real Estate Association, Statistics Canada

Your home also benefits from exceptionally favorable treatment under Canadian tax law. Because any gain between the purchase and sale price of your primary residence is tax-free, most owners have the opportunity to build substantial equity as their house gains in value, and their mortgage is paid down over the years. It's also quite a flexible investment since you can borrow against that equity to fund just about any worthwhile purpose such as educating your children. Ultimately, however, the greatest benefit of owning your own home is the security and peace of mind that comes from cost-free accommodation, especially in your later years. One of the surest roads to poverty for far too many people is to begin retirement as a tenant.

Owning isn't for everyone

Despite the advantages, some people's lifestyles might not suit the home-buying route. Even if it's a solid investment, people who travel a lot or who aren't planning on a family may prefer the hassle-free nature of rental accommodation. From a purely financial viewpoint, it's possible to make a case for renting instead of paying the mortgage if you direct the difference into higher-yielding investments. This is especially true in recent years given the relatively modest performance of the real estate sector.

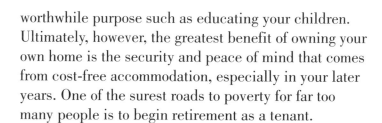

Principal payment:
The part of your mortgage payment that goes towards paying off the original loan.

If you want to assess the merits of owning a home versus renting on a purely financial basis, start by comparing monthly rental costs to the interest component of a monthly mortgage payment. The *principal payments* are considered the investment portion of the home ownership decision. The tradeoff to be evaluated, then, is the difference between putting available funds into a home as a down payment or to invest in mutual funds and RRSPs. Aside from the difficulty of evaluating the interest rate and rate of return assumptions used in your estimates, the forced savings aspect of a mortgage investment is often an easier discipline. If you are only interested in a house as an investment and aren't sure if it makes sense in your particular situation, there are software programs to help you with your calculations.

In short, owning a house is an ultimate dream for most Canadians because it's the foundation for family life, and it may be a better than average investment. But buying a house just for the investment benefits is probably a bad idea. The same holds for buying more house than you can afford just because you think house prices are going up. In the final analysis, a home is a place to live your life and you won't have much time to enjoy it if everything you earn is going to support the roof over your head.

Picking the right type of mortgage

In Canada, there are two types of mortgages: *conventional* and *insured* (also known as the *high-ratio* mortgage).

If you can afford it, the conventional mortgage is your best bet. To qualify, you must have a down payment equal to at least 25% of the purchase price of your home. If you haven't got the required down payment, you can still buy a house, but the law requires that your mortgage be insured through the Canada Mortgage and Housing Corporation (CMHC), a non-profit organization set up by the federal government to promote home ownership in Canada.

If your mortgage is CMHC insured, you can qualify for a loan of up to 95% of the value of the purchase price. This represents a high ratio of loan to

Conventional mortgage:
The prospective homeowner has at least 25% of the purchase price.

Insured or high-ratio mortgage:
The purchaser has a down payment of less than 25%.

value and thus it's sometimes known as the high-ratio
mortgage. High-ratio mortgages are popular with first-
time homebuyers who lack the means to scrape
together a down payment. In the early to mid-1980s,
when house prices were skyrocketing in major
Canadian centres, many people felt it made more sense
to take out a high-ratio mortgage than to patiently save
while house prices soared out of reach. And that
approach may have made sense since the increase in
equity in their homes more than offset the extra
cost of a CMHC-insured mortgage. In more
normal times, when real estate appreciates at a
more modest rate, the decision between buying
with less than 25% down or waiting until you
can afford a conventional mortgage is somewhat
more difficult.

**Preapproved
mortgage:**
*Where you know
how much you
can spend on a
house because
you've already
lined up the
money from your
financial
institution.*

The extra cost of a high-ratio mortgage will vary
depending on the extent to which your down
paymetn falls under the normal 25% mimimum
(see schedule opposite). There is also a maximum amount
of loan you can apply for, and this varies by region to
reflect the varying cost of housing in Canada.

Although CMHC is in the business of insuring high-
ratio mortgages, it's not in the business of lending money.
If you take out an insured mortgage, you will be dealing
as you normally would with a conventional lender such as
your bank or trust company.

While most lenders assume that the market will
ensure there isn't a significant discrepancy between what
you're going to pay for a property and its tru value, they
tend to behave a bit more conservatively if the size of the
mortgage exceeds 60% of the purchase price. In such

CMHC insurance fee

To have your mortgage insured by the Canadian Mortgage and Housing Corporation, you may pay an insurance premium, which is a percentage of the amount of your mortgage. You can pay the premium in full when you take out your mortgage or get a bit of a break on the interest rate. The following ranges and rates apply to resale homes, and you can obtain information on the full range of insurance fees by visiting the CMHC Web site at *www.chmc.ca/*. There is also an application fee.

Loan to value ratio		Insurance premimum*
Up to and including	65%	.50%
65.1% up to and including	75%	.75%
75.1% up to and including	80%	1.25%
80.1% up to and including	85%	2.00%
85.1% up to and including	90%	2.50%
90.1% up to and including	95%	3.75%

*A percentage of the mortgage amount

cases, a physical appraisal of property will be necessary to ensure your aren't being taken to the cleaners.

How much house can you afford?

It's easy to get frustrated if you go looking for your dream home before you figure out how much home you can afford. Prospective lenders will only be too happy to help you make an assessment and will often issue preapproved mortgages. These give you a much clearer idea of what you can afford and more flexibility in negotiating a purchase since you don't have to make your bid conditional upon financing. Lenders use the same GDS and TDS measures described in the previous chapter as the basis for determining how much mortgage you qualify for.

A quick affordability test

Another quick way to estimate the affordability of a home is to multiply your gross family income by 2.5. This means, on average, that a family with a gross annual income of $55,000 can buy a home valued at $137,500.

No matter how you or your lenders calculate the size of the mortgage you can handle, remember that only you can determine how big a part of your income can be devoted to shelter. GDS, TDS and the 2.5 family income test are at best rough measures. They don't take into account significant expenses such as child care that can affect the amount of money you can afford to spend on shelter. Neither do they take into account the cost of basic annual upkeep, estimated at about 1% of the purchase price, let alone any major repairs, redecorating or renovation plans you might consider important.

By the same token, you may be an urban survivalist who spends far less than the average person on entertainment or transportation, and can afford more than these basic tests would indicate. The key is to not treat credit approval as a contest or confuse the ability to qualify for credit as the need to take advantage of it.

Choosing your mortgage

Once you've determined how much debt your family can afford, the next step is to choose the right type of mortgage. You'll have three basic decisions to make.

Open versus closed mortgages

With an *open mortgage*, you are free to pay off the full
amount of your mortgage or refinance it, at any time
and without penalty. In contrast, with a *closed
mortgage*, you are locked in for the full term of
the mortgage and paying it off early or
refinancing it attracts a severe penalty, usually
equivalent to at least two months of interest
payments.

Open mortgage:
*You can pay off
as much of the
mortgage —
even the full
amount — at any
time and without
penalty.*

An open mortgage might appeal to you if
interest rates are expected to keep declining
and you're reluctant to lock into what may be an
unnecessarily high rate. As expected, there is a price to
be paid for such flexibility, and lately it's been up to
1% more than a comparable closed mortgage. In an
attempt to attract borrowers who are temporarily
uncertain where interest rates are headed, most banks
have developed a popular new variation of the
open mortgage in the last few years: the six-
month convertible mortgage. With the added
benefit of an attractive interest rate, it's
designed to allow you to bide your time until
interest rates appear to be heading up, at which
point you can lock in. Most convertible
mortgages can be renewed indefinitely, usually
without a renewal fee, until you are comfortable making
a commitment.

Closed mortgage:
*You are bound to
a set rate for the
full term. A stiff
penalty is
charged to pay
off this type of
mortgage early
or to refinance.*

Fixed versus variable interest rates

You will also have the choice of locking into a fixed

interest rate or letting your interest rate rise and fall with trends in the market. Variable rate mortgages are less expensive because you assume a bit of risk that the bank would otherwise assume. In return, the required interest rate is a bit lower, which usually results in lower total interest payments over the lifetime of the mortgage.

The fact is, most people live on a fairly tight budget and can't take chances with significant fluctuations in their monthly payments. Interest rates have been known to spike upwards in times of high inflation as they did from 1980 to 1982 when the interest rate for a five-year mortgage went to 18.04% from 14.52%. While interest rates generally have been falling since the early 1980s, you run the risk of your monthly payments rising if you choose a variable interest rate.

Short-term versus long-term mortgages
The same kind of guessing game enters into your decision between a short- and long-term mortgage. Terms usually range from six months to 10 years. Generally, the interest rate charged by the bank rises in direct proportion to the length of the term. That's simply because the bank takes on more risk. If you lock in for a five-year term and rates subsequently rise, the bank will have lost an opportunity to lend that money for a higher return. And the bank will have to wait a full five years to set things right. On the other hand, if you opted for a one-year term, and rates subsequently increased, the bank would not have to wait nearly so long to renew your mortgage and relend that

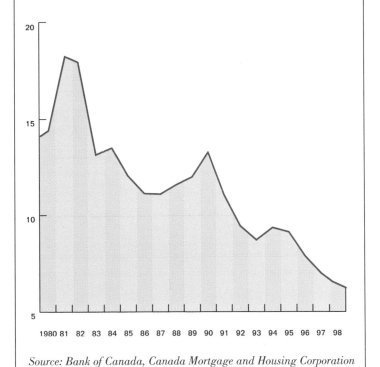

Interest rates for a five-year mortgage

Interest rates have come down substantially since the 1980s and early 1990s, making mortgage costs more affordable and home ownership attractive.

Source: Bank of Canada, Canada Mortgage and Housing Corporation

money at higher rates. Generally, the longer the term of the mortgage, the greater the degree of risk assumed by the bank with respect to subsequent rate changes. As such, longer-term mortgages usually carry a higher interest rate than equivalent short-term mortgages.

If you can afford a bit of volatility in your monthly

payments, then short-term mortgages will save you money in the long-term. The danger, of course, is that your mortgage will come up for renewal during a period of sustained high interest rates.

Choosing your repayment options

Although that initial mortgage payment is usually big enough to put a lump in your throat, with the passage of time and a few pay increases you will probably find that it's not nearly so onerous. Eventually, your mortgage payment will consume a smaller portion of your take-home pay.

As a result, it's surprisingly easy to get complacent. That's a big mistake. Although you might get to the point where your mortgage feels more comfortable, you should never cease to regard it as an income-devouring beast that must be vanquished. In the next section, we'll take a look at each of the factors that determine the size of your monthly payment as well as some strategies to help you reduce your total mortgage costs.

The last few years have witnessed increasing competition between lenders in the mortgage market, and thanks to the advent of increasingly powerful software programs, all of the banks and trust companies have been making their products more flexible, with a growing range of prepayment options. Their net effect has been to give you unprecedented ability to pay off your mortgage early. While the wrinkles vary from one institution to another, there are several basic features to look for.

Lenders offer many options to help you pay off your home early.

Annual lump-sum payments

Most mortgages now give you the chance to make
lump-sum annual payments against the principal —
usually in an amount equal to 10% to 15% of the
outstanding balance or the original mortgage amount.
This may not seem like a big advantage when you first
take out the mortgage, but the flexibility can let
you make the most of an unexpected windfall
such as an inheritance, tax refund or bonus.

Prepayment option:
*A feature of
many mortgages
that lets you
increase or
double up your
payments.*

When your mortgage is up for renewal and
you decide to stay with the same institution,
your prepayment privilege may apply to the
original principal of your mortgage. For example, if you
originally borrowed $100,000 for your mortgage and at
renewal the principal stood at $80,000, you could
prepay up to $10,000 each year — and not $8,000. If

you consider switching to a new financial institution, weigh this factor before making your decision.

Variable monthly payments

Most mortgages let you increase the size of your monthly payment whenever you can, whether it's doubling up the normal payment or paying whatever additional chunks of cash you can scrounge up from time to time. If your mortgage is of a longer term — say five years — you probably will find the monthly mortgage payment more affordable as time goes by, especially if your income goes up. In that case, this feature will prove a very effective way to reduce your mortgage costs.

Frequency of payments

Most mortgages also give you the choice of making your payments monthly, every two weeks or weekly, a handy option depending on how often you and your spouse get paid. Many institutions make a big deal out of the money you can save by paying your mortgage weekly rather than monthly. While you'll save money, the reason is not so much the increased frequency of payments as the fact that you will be paying more against the principal each month. For example, if instead of paying $1,000 a month, you decide to pay $250 a week, you will indeed be taking a bigger bite out of your mortgage each year. The reason, of course, is that there are 4.33 weeks in the average month, not four. As a result, you would pay the equivalent of $1,082.50 a month. In addition, your mortgage holder is being repaid sooner, so the balance of your mortgage decreases much faster.

Taming your mortgage

There are ways to lighten your mortgage load and save thousands in the process. This table compares the effects of making the regular payments on a $150,000 mortgage, making one double payment per year, shortening the amortization period by five years, and making a single 10% lump-sum payment. The calculations are based on an interest rate of 7% and, unless otherwise stated, the amortization period is 25 years.

Option	Monthly payments	Total interest paid*	Amount saved	Number of years to pay off mortgage
25-year amortization period	$1,050.63	$165,184	$0	25
one double payment per year**	$1,138.18	$131,483	$33,701	20.61
20-year amortization	$1,153.97	$126,951	$38,233	20
one 10% ($15,000) prepayment on 25-year amortization	$1,050.63	$114,900	$50,284	19.82
one 10% ($15,000) prepayment on 20-year amortization	$1,153.97	$92,857	$72,327	16.45

rounded to the nearest dollar
**extra payment is spread evenly over 12 months.*

47

Choosing an amortization period

Unlike the term of the mortgage, which is the period of time until renewal, the amortization period is how long it will take to completely pay off your mortgage. It's also the period on which the size of your payments is based. And without exception, the longer the amortization period, the smaller the monthly payment required. With a 25-year amortization period, the amount you pay each month will be significantly smaller than, for example, a 20-year amortization period, in which you have to pay back the amount you borrowed in 80% of the time. However, built into those smaller payments in the 25-year mortgage is a significantly greater amount of interest. That's simply because you will have ended up borrowing the money for five more years.

While prepayment options have the net effect of shortening your amortization period, it's a good idea to specifically choose the shortest possible amortization period you can afford. Through complacency, many people just allow the amortization to start out at 25 years and reduce by one year at each anniversary of the mortgage. In the end, you can save thousands of dollars in interest by shortening the amortization period. To calculate your mortgage payments under different interest rates, amortization periods and payment frequency, see the mortgage calculator in the appendix, page 213.

It pays to shop around

The one factor we haven't mentioned is the importance of shopping around. You might wonder why it's so

important when the big banks publish virtually
identical interest rates for the same term and when
their products contain remarkably similar prepayment
options and other features.

The fact is, banks make money on the
difference between what they pay in interest to
their depositors and what they charge in
interest to their borrowers. Posted deposit and
loan rates reflect this reality and the spreads
between them are usually about 2% depending
on the term.

Posted rate:
*Advertised
interest rate,
usually can be
negotiated down
or up by about
0.5%.*

Sometimes, however, there are temporary imbalances
between an institution's deposits and the corresponding
amount of loans for a given term. In such cases, the lender
may be more eager to lend out money for a better rate —
sometimes up to three quarters of a percent lower than the
posted rate depending on the term. If negotiating a lower
rate may not seem worth the trouble, you might be
interested to know that on a $100,000 mortgage with a
five-year term, the difference between an interest rate of
7% and 6.25% amounts to a savings of nearly $14,000
over a 25-year amortization period.

A mortgage broker can help

While mortgage brokers have traditionally specialized
in securing financing for substandard or unusual risks,
they are beginning to play a larger role in matching the
needs of everyday borrowers. In fact, the mortgages
they offer are the very same ones you get directly from
the banks and trust companies except that mortgage
brokers can get lower rates for you. Because mortgage
brokers deal in volume, they can usually extract

concessions that are passed on to their clients. Most mortgage brokers won't charge you for their services because they get a finder's fee from the lending institution.

What about mom and dad?
It's natural for parents or other close relatives to help their loved ones. Perhaps your parents have offered to give you a mortgage or to help you save for a down payment. Before you make up your mind, ask a few important questions.

Is your relative able to loan you the money without significantly altering their lifestyle? Could your relative need or want to ask for repayment before the term is up? Will the mortgage or loan damage in any way your relationship?

If you've determined that a mortgage from a family member is the way to go, make sure you have the correct documents drawn up by a lawyer. Also, you might want to have an accountant act as an intermediary, to accept, record and forward the monthly payments to the mortgage holder, so there can be no misunderstanding about the amount and timeliness of the payments. As well, have your accountant draw up an annual mortgage statement and forward a copy to you and your relative.

Chapter 5

Life insurance – why you need it

It's important to adequately insure your life,
livelihood and major assets to protect your family.

Life insurance provides for your loved ones

Most people don't like to think about insurance, especially life insurance. Maybe it's because they don't want to dwell on the possibility of an early death. Whatever the reason, unless you are independently wealthy, failing to give careful consideration to the kind and amount of insurance you need can have tragic consequences.

The purpose of this book is to help you formulate a plan to achieve financial independence and security. But as you know, achieving these goals is a long-term process. Your plan assumes that you will have many years to reach your goals. But what if you don't live long enough to see it through? Or become disabled, get sued, or see your assets go up in smoke? The point of insurance is to make sure that the lives of you and your loved ones will go on as planned if the unthinkable happens.

So far, all our suggestions for wise financial planning have been based on the assumption of continuous employment income. But what would happen if you were no longer around? The fact is, unless you had adequate life insurance, your family would have some serious adjustments to make.

Deciding what you're worth

How much do you need? That depends on a number of factors including your present net worth, the number and age of your dependents and your spouse's employment status. Never guess at such an important figure. Also remember that, like the larger process of financial planning, insurance planning is a continual process. You should review your circumstances at least once a year, or whenever there's a major change such as an addition to your family, to ensure that all your risks are adequately covered.

It's often wise to buy more than you need at the time. If you have one child but might have more, it could make sense to buy more coverage now. That's because, unlike other financial products, your ability to buy insurance depends on more than just how much you're willing to spend. It also depends on your age and the state of your health when you buy it. And while most of us tend to regard ourselves as immortal when we're young, physical health rarely improves over time. A lot of Canadians become uninsurable during their working lives and can't get the coverage they want when they really need it. As we'll see in the next chapter, there are ways to avoid this problem.

Life insurance worksheet

The worksheet on page 54 will help you develop a clearer picture of how much life insurance you and your spouse need.

Life Insurance Worksheet

Assets Available	If you die	If your spouse dies
cash	$_____	$_____
personal life insurance	$_____	$_____
group life insurance	$_____	$_____
CPP/QPP death benefits*	$_____	$_____
RPP death benefits	$_____	$_____
RRSP assets to liquidate	$_____	$_____
investment portfolio to liquidate	$_____	$_____
other assets to be sold	$_____	$_____
Total assets available (A):	$_____	$_____

*Benefit amounts are revised regularly. For the latest CPP benefits, check with Human Resources Development Canada (Tel: 1-800-277-9914; Web site www.hrdc-drhc.gc.ca/) for the latest QPP benefits, contact the Régis des rentes de Québec (Tel: 1-800-463-5185; Web site: www.gouv.quc.ca/).

1 These include things such as final medical bills, funderal costs, current unpaid bills, bank or other outstanding loans, unpaid property taxes, probate costs, legal and executor fees and unpaid income tax.

2 This fund is an important part of a life insurance plan. The fund will cancel a mortgage balance and all future interest payments, help pay for educating any dependent children, and

Estate Obligations at Death	$_____	$_____
last expenses[1]	$_____	$_____
mortgage cancellations	$_____	$_____
education emergency fund[2]	$_____	$_____
Total Cash Needed (B)	$_____	$_____
Income Needs of Survivor(s)		
required gross monthly income (generally 70% to 80% of current income)[3]	$_____	$_____
subtract: CPP/QPP survivor benefits*	$_____	$_____
subtract: CPP/QPP orphan benefits*	$_____	$_____
Net Monthly Income Required (C):	$_____	$_____
Total Annual Income Capital Needed (D): (C x 12)	$_____	$_____
TOTAL ADDITIONAL CAPITAL NEEDED (B + D - A):	$_____	$_____

give dependent survivors something to draw on in case of serious illness, accident or other emergency.

3 This may include money needed to see surviving dependents through to the time they graduate from college or university. The surviving spouse may also require income. If both parents die, the guardian may require funds to raise the children.

What kind of life insurance do you need?

There are all kinds of policies out there.
Here's how to choose the coverage that's best for
you and your family.

Match needs against choices

Now that you've solved the most important question about life insurance — how much you need — the next step is to find the type of insurance that best suits your individual circumstances.

There are essentially two basic types of life insurance: *term* insurance and *permanent* or *whole life* insurance. To determine which type is best for you, ask yourself how long you'll need it, how much you can afford to spend, and what you expect it do for you. For example, do you want it to strictly cover the risk of premature death or do you want to have something to show for your premiums whether you live or die?

Term insurance

Term insurance is the most basic and least-expensive type of insurance because it's priced simply to cover the risk of you dying. A policy that pays $100,000 in the event of your death might cost $500 a year. Like a lottery, your $500 premium goes into a big pot along with the premiums of thousands of other people. The few individuals who die win the big payoff and the ones who don't probably won't complain about losing the lottery. The insurance company can't know who will die in any given year, but it knows, statistically, how many people of a certain age group will die in a certain year and prices its premiums accordingly. The idea is to charge enough in premiums to cover the expected number of death benefits, plus leave a little for profit.

Term insurance: Life insurance that pays a set amount should you die within the specified period. The typical term is five years, and many term policies are renewable, at higher rates.

58

How much life insurance Canadians own

Individual life insurance	$870.7 billion
Group life insurance	$881.6 billion
Average amount owned by each individual	$107,900

Source: Canadian Association of Insurance & Financial Advisors

How much it costs

While term insurance is by far the most affordable type for younger people, it becomes more expensive as you get older. That's because the price is directly linked to the number of people who will die at any given age and with a few exceptions, the likelihood of dying increases with each passing year. As people reach their late 50s, term insurance becomes very expensive, something the average person should consider only if there'll be dependents at home or in school.

Although term insurance becomes more expensive with age, it's usually priced in age bands that guarantee a set premium for the period of the coverage. This means that the premium won't increase during the term you choose. Usually, term policies are also guaranteed renewable when their current term expires, although at that point the cost of insurance will undoubtedly rise. Most term policies give premiums for all age groups, so you'll have an idea of how much more in premiums you'll have to pay when you move into the next age category.

When shopping for term insurance, it's important to consider how long you'll likely need it and the total cost of insurance during that period. The set annual premiums for a 20-year term policy will undoubtedly be higher than the annual premiums payable on a 10-year term policy. But if you are going to need insurance for at least 20 years, the 20 year-term might be a better buy than two successive 10-year policies.

Permanent insurance

Permanent or whole life insurance is designed to remain in force for your entire lifetime. While the premiums for term policies are more expensive the older you are when you take them out, premiums for permanent insurance are designed to stay the same for your entire life. As you might expect, the premium you pay is higher than term insurance in the early years, and less than term insurance in the later years. Overall, however, you'll generally pay much more over your lifetime for permanent insurance than for an equivalent amount of term insurance.

Permanent or whole life insurance: Provides coverage for your entire life and pays a predetermined benefit when you die.

One of the reasons for this is obvious. A permanent policy will eventually pay a death benefit, while term insurance only pays if you die while you're covered. But there are other reasons permanent policies are more expensive. One is that a portion of the premiums you pay is directed into a reserve which provides other options that don't come with a term policy. You can use it to buy annuities for retirement income, you can stop premium payments and buy less coverage, or you can even borrow against the reserve at the interest rates specified in the policy. You may also qualify for dividends, which are partial refunds of your premium, if the insurance company is able to generate sufficient returns on the extra money in the policy's reserve.

Remember, though, that there is a cost to all these nifty features. With a permanent policy, you're paying for more than the strict cost of life insurance. You're getting some potentially valuable benefits in return, but the insurance company is also keeping its fair share of the additional premium.

An insurance agent may tell you that it makes no more sense to buy term versus whole life than it does to rent instead of buy your house. Intuitively, it makes more sense to own rather than rent. But life insurance may be one area where renting is the wiser option. If you have the financial discipline, it often makes more sense to buy term and invest the money you'll save on lower premiums in wealth-generating assets.

Annuity:
A contract that guarantees you a series of payments in exchange for your lump sum investment.

Reserve:
A feature of whole life insurance that gives you options for such things as buying an annuity for retirement or to stop premium payments.

Hybrid insurance products

When interest rates began to rise in the late 1970s, insurance companies found that the guaranteed cash values in their whole life policies were beginning to look rather uncompetitive. As a result, more and more potential customers tried to achieve financial security by buying term and investing the difference in higher-yielding alternatives such as GICs. To make permanent insurance policies more attractive, insurers began to introduce

Universal life:
Consists of term life insurance and an investment account.

61

policies whose cash values were based on their underlying investments. Basically, there are two types of such policies: *universal life* and *variable life*.

Universal life

This type of policy has two distinct parts: term life insurance and an investment account. A portion of each is used to cover administrative expenses and the so-called mortality factor of dying when you aren't supposed to. The balance is credited to an investment account which is invested in the *money market*.

Money market: Segment of the market where you can trade short-term investments such as federal government T-bills, commercial paper and guaranteed investment certificates.

The separate investment account gives the policy some flexibility. Premiums can be increased or decreased, paid when due, or whenever the policyholder wants, as long as there is enough money in the account to cover mortality costs and expenses. You can even decide to increase the death benefit amount within certain limits.

While some would argue that it's better to keep your insurance and investment objectives entirely separate, there are some unique advantages to this hybrid universal life product. For instance, in addition to giving you a tax-free death benefit, it allows you to shelter some of your investment income from tax.

Variable life

With the rise of mutual fund investing, insurance companies began to offer a second type of hybrid policy called variable life. Like universal life, it consists of two components: one for insurance, one for investments. However, there are some important differences. For starters, the death benefit is funded not by term insurance but by permanent whole life insurance with a fixed premium. In addition, the investment component offers considerably more flexibility. With a variable life plan, the value of the investment component depends on the performance of a *segregated fund*. A typical segregaged fund is similar to a mutual fund, execept that you are guaranteed to get back what you put into it after typically 10 years or if you die. Most policies allow you to choose between segregated stock, bond and balanced funds. And, similar to universal life products, much of the investment gain is sheltered from tax.

Segregated funds: Similar to mutual funds, seg funds promise to return at least 75% of your money at a future maturity date or on your death.

Variable life: Comprises fixed-premium whole life policy and investment account that you can direct.

Many people get sold on the idea of universal and variable life products because they like the idea of saving tax. But as in any other "investment," that shouldn't be the deciding factor in your purchase. Generally speaking, you should only be looking at these products if you need the insurance and you already make maximum use of far more effective tax shelters such as your primary residence and your RRSP.

Tax shelter: An investment that may reduce or deay payment of taxes.

Can you get optimum rates?

If you've ever looked at life insurance tables, you may remember that, aside from your age and gender, there's another key factor that helps determine how much premium you'll pay. The factor is smoking. Generally

Should you insure the kids?

Since the parents pay the bills, insuring your children isn't necessary.

All you need is enough to cover funeral expenses. A policy through work or an association will likely provide enough money to cover funeral expenses.

speaking, smokers pay more for the same coverage than non-smokers. The reason is simply that non-smokers usually live longer than smokers, and the insurer stands to collect more in premiums before it has to make a payout.

Some policies may also charge lower premiums if you're classed as a non-drinker. In the insurance company's eyes, "non-drinker" may not mean that you never have a glass or wine or beer. Rather, it's meant to distinguish the "real drinkers" from those who enjoy the occasional social drink. Again, people with healthier lifestyles present a lower risk to insurers. If you're a moderate or non-drinker, it's wise to ask if the insurance company can give you a break on your premium.

Chapter 7

Other types of insurance

Arranging your affairs adequately for the
possibility of personal disability,
damage to your home or car, and, of course death,
will save your family undue hardship.

Disability insurance protects your ability to earn income

While dying without adequate life insurance would no doubt throw a wrench into your financial plans, there's another great peril. It's loss of income due to disability. In fact, from a financial perspective, disability can be worse than death. Not only does it result in a loss of income, it's often accompanied by additional medical and other expenses.

Few people would think twice about buying insurance for their car or house. Yet for some strange reason, many of us don't bother to protect the most important asset of all and that, of course, is the ability to earn the income that paid for those possessions. Equally puzzling, we are much more inclined to insure against our premature death than the possibility of becoming disabled.

The fact is, a 20-year-old male is about three times as likely to become disabled for three months or more than to die before age 65. For a 35-year-old woman, the odds are seven to one. And on a broader scale, more than two million Canadians of working age are disabled.

Given these statistics, it's no surprise that disability insurance is costly. The amount you pay will vary depending on your age, occupation and amount and type of coverage. But in almost every case, you can't afford to be without this type of insurance. Let's have a look at some of the factors that will determine the cost and quality of your coverage.

Beware of how 'disability' is defined

The definition of disability is one of the most important features of your policy because it can have a major impact when you make a claim.

Own occupation

This is the preferred and standard definition of disability with most individual policies. It considers you to be disabled if you can't perform the regular duties of your own occupation. For example, even if a brain surgeon with an injured hand is able to find a job teaching medicine at the local university, benefits are still payable.

Any occupation

This is the more restrictive definition, and it's the one usually found in company-sponsored or group disability contracts. If, after receiving benefits for two years, you are able to perform another occupation for which you are reasonably suited by virtue of training, education or experience, the insurer can stop payments.

Benefit periods vary widely

Most policies pay benefits, as long as you are disabled, for up to two years, five years, age 65 or for life. As you might expect, the longer the benefit period, the higher the premium. Although disabilities that last more than two years are relatively rare, most people prefer to pay for the peace of mind that comes with coverage to at least age 65.

Consider an extended waiting period
This is the period you have to wait before you can start receiving benefits, and it usually varies from 30 days to six months. If you can afford to look after yourself for a few months in the event of a disability, you can save a lot of money on premiums. Insurance companies pay a lot of claims for relatively short-term disabilities. In fact, even in the event of a serious medical emergency such as a heart attack, patients are usually back at work within a couple months. If you can afford a longer waiting period, you stand to save a significant amount in premiums.

How much disability insurance do you need?

If you make $2,500 a month, that's roughly how much disability insurance you will need to fully replace your income. You aren't likely to get that much from a disability policy, though, because insurers are concerned that a full benefit would effectively remove any incentive to return to work. So they'll usually pay a benefit no greater than 70% of your normal income. That's not as bad as it sounds, however, because if you are paying the premiums on your disability policy with after-tax dollars, any benefits you collect are received tax-free. Of course, the value of your disability income can be eaten away by inflation. For this reason, most insurance policies offer a cost-of-living benefit for an additional fee.

Other sources of disability insurance

One of the primary reasons most Canadians don't buy individual disability coverage is the perception that they are adequately covered through other sources. There is some truth to this, although the degree of risk varies widely depending on individual circumstances. Here's a quick review of the employer- and government-sponsored programs that may come into play if you're absent from work for an extended time due to illness or injury.

Group insurance

Most Canadians are covered through employer-sponsored insurance programs that include disability coverage. Quite often, however, the maximum amount of your benefit will depend not on what you need, but on the number of people in your group. If you work for a small company, the amount of coverage may be inadequate.

What's more, the definition of disability in group contracts is almost always the less favorable "any occupation" definition. And, of course, your coverage terminates when you leave the group.

One of the benefits of group disability coverage is that, depending on the number of employees in your company, you may be able to get substantial amounts of coverage without having to prove your state of health. This might benefit you if you are in poor health. In contrast, individual disability coverage requires medical approval for any amount of coverage.

Group benefits are taxable in your hands if the employer pays the cost of coverage. If you pay the premiums they are not.

Canada Pension Plan

You have to be permanently and totally disabled to collect the maximum CPP disability benefit and it's hard for most people to qualify. If you can, it's payable after six months until age 65 or prior recovery. Most group insurance contracts will reduce their benefit by the amount you get from CPP. Individual contracts will not.

Workers compensation

Employers in Canada are required to pay premiums into the various provincial workers compensation schemes to cover absence from work or disability due to work-related injury or illness. The rules and benefits of workers compensation are set by each province. Generally speaking, workers compensation covers blue-collar or hourly workers as well as white-collar or salaried workers up to the executive level.

However, if you are an executive working for a manufacturing company, you may be covered by workers compensation without realizing it. If in doubt, check with your employer.

Property and casualty insurance

Now that you've considered the insurance you need to protect your income, it's time to consider how best to protect your physical assets. Your home and car probably represent a substantial portion of your net worth. Losing either one of them might cause serious hardship. What's more, each of these assets exposes you to the risk of injuring others and thus potentially damaging lawsuits. As a result, comprehensive property and casualty insurance is one of the cornerstones of sound financial planning.

Homeowner's coverage

Whether you own or rent, this is coverage you can't afford to be without. Basically, it insures the contents and structure of your residence in an amount specified by the policy. Invariably, this will be less than the real estate value of the house because, even if your house burns to the ground, you will still have the land. There are three basic types of home-owner's insurance policies, and they offer varying degrees of protection.

Named perils:
Basic calamities such as fire are usually specified individually in the policy.

The standard or most basic policy only covers you for *named perils* that are listed in the policy. You will always be covered if your house goes up in smoke but you won't likely find sewer backup as one of the named perils. As you might expect, this is the least expensive kind of homeowner's policy.

All-risk:
Covers all perils except those stated as exclusions.

Comprehensive:
Similar to all-risk coverage, but has fewer exceptions.

For about 15% more premium, you can get what's known as an *all-risk* policy. This type covers you for any kind of loss except those that are specifically mentioned as exclusions in the policy. It's a much safer bet since you get to identify in advance each of the specific occurrences for which you won't be covered.

If you are interested in maximum peace of mind, it might make sense to get the *comprehensive* policy, which typically costs an additional 15% in premium. It, too, is an all-risk policy except it has fewer exclusions. It will usually contain accidental coverage — handy if you drop a hot iron on the carpet. It will also cover you for things that mysteriously disappear and provide higher limits for things like camera equipment and jewelry.

The other important part of the homeowner's policy, no matter what kind of policy you buy, is liability coverage. This is the type of protection you need if the paper carrier slips on your porch and ends up with a broken leg. Most policies now contain at least $1 million in liability coverage, but it's a relatively inexpensive component in the homeowner's policy. Whatever amount you choose you should maintain an adequate level of coverage.

Liability coverage: Protects you if you hurt someone in a car accident or if a person slips and falls on your porch.

Automobile coverage

Like homeowner's coverage, car insurance is fairly standard from one insurer to another. It's the cost that varies significantly. How much you will pay depends on several factors including the driver's age, years of driving experience, driving record and the cost and type of vehicle. Basically, your automobile policy can be broken down into four types of coverage.

- **Collision insurance:** covers your car for damage in case you bang into another vehicle or stationary object. Normally, you pay the first $250 to $300 of damage but if you can afford to raise this deductible, you can save on premiums.

- **Comprehensive insurance:** covers the other things that can happen to your car including fire and theft.

- **Personal accident insurance:** covers any medical expenses that aren't covered by your provincial health plan plus funeral expenses. Most policies also provide a small disability pension if you are unable to work as a result of the accident.

- **Liability insurance:** protects you if you injure someone else or cause damage to other vehicles or property in an accident. It's illegal to drive without it. Most policies contain at least $1 million in liability coverage.

Why you may need extra liability insurance

Chances are, you'll be covered for at least $1 million in liability coverage through your automobile and homeowner's polices. However, court awards are continuing to increase and there may be particular circumstances where neither of these policies comes into play. If you have a relatively high net worth or higher than normal degree of exposure to risk — let's say you own a boat or airplane — it's probably a good idea to get extra liability coverage. Basically, there are three types.

- **Umbrella coverage:** pays any liability claims that exceed the limits in your other policies up to a maximum of about $6 million. Because it only comes into play if the coverage in your automobile and homeowner's policies falls short, it's relatively inexpensive — approximately $150 for each $1 million of coverage.

- **Directors and officers coverage:** designed for directors and officers of organizations who might be held personally responsible for the organization's negligence. Most large companies take out specific insurance to cover their senior people, but many small companies and volunteer and charitable organizations do not. If you act as a director for an organization, it pays to find out if you are covered by directors and officers insurance, no matter how small your risk might appear to be.

- **Professional liability:** created for lawyers, engineers, doctors, accountants and other professionals. If you fall into this category and are unsure if you have this coverage, it's wise to check with your employer or professional association. Remember, too, that you can even be sued for professional advice given free of charge outside the workplace. Litigation is on the rise in our society, and the sad fact is that an engineer who offers casual advice to a neighbor on the construction of a deck may face some risk.

Chapter 8

Wills and power of attorney

Ensure your wishes can be carried out before adversity has a chance to strike.

Why you need a will

Like life and disability insurance, wills don't evoke a lot of excitement for most people.

But by having a will prepared now, you'll gain peace of mind that your wishes will be carried out. You'll also spare your family considerable financial and emotional pain.

If you die *intestate* — without a will — the laws in your province set out how your assets will be distributed. In such cases, some or all of your assets could go to people you do not want as beneficiaries. More importantly, if you have dependent children, you may want to specify in your will who you want to act as their guardian.

Intestate:
Dying without a will.

Codicil:
Amendment to a will.

Beware, though, that in some provinces the courts are not bound to comply with your wishes for a guardian.

While some provinces consider a hand-written will valid, it's in your family's best interest to have a will drawn up with the help of a lawyer or, if you live in Quebec, with assistance from a notary public. If you have considerable assets or run a business, you may also want to consult a tax advisor. Typically, a lawyer will charge a couple hundred dollars for a standard will. As with other components of your financial plan, you should review your will every year or so, and certainly keep abreast of tax changes that can affect your assets. If you want to make a change to your will, give your lawyer your new instructions to draw up a *codicil*, which is legalese for an amendment to a will.

When it comes to the welfare of your family, don't put someone else in the driver's seat.

Arrange a power of attorney

It's understandable to not think about power of attorney until you're much older, but you'll do yourself and your family a big favor by taking care of this now. If there's just one income earner in your family, or if you rely on two incomes to make ends meet, a power of attorney will enable your family to manage their affairs if you're unable.

Essentially, power of attorney is a legal document that gives the person you name authority to make certain decisions on your behalf, usually if you become mentally or physically incapable. Many people name their spouse or someone close whose judgment and honesty they trust.

Power of attorney: Give signing power over your affairs to a person you trust in case an accident or other circumstance leaves you unable to manage your own affairs.

There are two types of power of attorney: financial and personal. You can state exactly what the person can do on your behalf, such as sell a particular investment or arrange for a certain type of medical care. As well, you can specify how long the power of attorney is in force, such as five years after you sign it. Lawyers typically charge around $75 to prepare a standard power of attorney.

Defining your investment goals

Your goals, stage in life, and risk tolerance are all part of your investment decisions.

Getting down to the basics

There was a day when many Canadians could retire comfortably if their homes were paid for and they received a tidy pension, preferably one that was indexed to inflation. Unfortunately, this isn't the case for most people now. Government programs such as the Canada and Quebec pension plans are vulnerable. At the same time, fewer Canadians belong to employer-sponsored pension plans. Those who do are increasingly expected to make decisions about how their contributions are invested. For all these reasons, having a basic understanding of investment fundamentals is more important than ever.

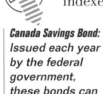

Canada Savings Bond:
Issued each year by the federal government, these bonds can be cashed in at any time for their face value.

Treasury bill (T-bill):
Short-term government bond that doesn't pay interest but which is sold at a discount to its maturity value.

Principal:
The original amount you invest, also called your capital.

Deciding how and where to invest your money starts with a fundamental examination of what you want your money to do for you. And this depends on the goals you have set, your stage in life and your income needs. Of course, you must also consider your personal tolerance for risk and your own objectives. For example, a suitable investment for retirement may not be at all appropriate for funding a university education. Although each of your investments will vary depending on your needs, chances are you will select them to meet one or more of these objectives: safety of capital, income and growth.

Safety of capital

If you have a specific short-term goal in mind, such as saving for the down payment on a house, your main

concern is keeping your principal intact. Investments
such as treasury bills, GICs and Canada Savings Bonds
(CSBs) are highly liquid and very safe, and you know
the money will be there when you need it. The
downside of such investments, of course, is that the
longer you hold them, the more their buying power is
diminished by inflation.

Income

If you are prepared to accept some risk that
your principal might decline in value, and are
willing to live with a bit less *liquidity*, then
there are many investments that can generate a
higher rate of return than GICs and CSBs.
Examples include mutual funds that invest in
medium- and long-term bonds or in stocks that
pay fixed or high *dividends*, such as *preferred
shares*. Traditionally, financial advisors
recommend income-producing investments to
seniors who need a reliable stream of cash to
meet day-to-day living expenses. However, even
younger people can benefit from having some
income-producing investments in their
portfolios to reduce their overall risk.

Growth

Short of starting and building a successful
business, receiving an inheritance or winning
the lottery, there's only one way to accumulate
substantial wealth in your lifetime: by devoting
a large portion of your investments to growth
assets such as common stocks and equity

Liquidity:
The ability to get
fast access to
your money.

Dividend:
The money
companies pay
from their
earnings to
shareholders.
Dividends to
preferred
shareholders are
usually for a set
amount and
normally are paid
before any
dividends are
declared for
common
shareholders.

Preferred shares:
A type of
income-
producing
security whose
owners usually
receive fixed
dividends.

mutual funds. These assets can provide income through dividends, which represent your share of the profits of the companies you invest in. As well, when the value of your stock or mutual fund unit rises and you sell your holdings, you receive a *capital gain* on your investment.

Capital gain: *The money you make when you sell an investment for more than you paid for it.*

What type of investment is right for you?

While there is no single right answer to this question, there are two primary considerations: your tolerance for risk and your age. Generally, they go hand in hand. Most financial advisors recommend a relatively aggressive approach in the early part of your working life and a more conservative approach when retirement is just around the corner.

In your 20s to 40s

Most people in their 20s, 30s and 40s try to build a strong financial base for retirement by focusing on investments that provide returns significantly above inflation. Because you have time to ride out market fluctuations, you can afford to take some risk and profit from the potentially higher returns of equities.

When you're 50

In your 50s, retirement is not far off and likely you're more concerned about an economic downturn that could reduce the value of your investments for a sustained time. This is the age when many Canadians begin to rebalance their portfolios in favor of fixed-income investments like bonds.

In your 60s

Once you reach age 60, your investment horizon is relatively short, although people today are living longer than before and sometimes pursue new "careers" after retirement. At this point, all your wise investing should mean you are very close to reaching your financial goals. Now is usually the time to protect all that precious retirement income. The emphasis usually is on safety of capital and, ideally, income that can at least keep pace with inflation. Accordingly, investments such as GICs, short-term bond funds, and mortgage funds arc often popular choices at this stage in life. However, since you may have 20 years or more to enjoy retirement, you will still want some growth in your portfolio to help ensure your money lasts at least as long as you do.

Of course, these generalizations illustrate the importance of how much of your assets should be placed in each of the three main investment groups, according to your age. Your situation may be very different from most people's. If you'll be well taken care of by your employer and government-sponsored pension plans, you might decide to keep your own retirement savings invested primarily in growth-oriented investments until

Growth-oriented asset mix by age group

Age	Cash	Income	Growth
up to 50	5%	25%	70%
50 to 60	10%	45%	45%
60s	5%	60%	25%

Asset mix:
The proportion of your entire holdings in each of the three investment categories: cash, fixed-income and growth.

you stop working. In fact, with the flexibility of RRIFs, which we discuss in Chapter 20, many of today's seniors continue to keep a substantial portion of their assets invested in growth investments like stocks well into retirement.

Chapter 10

Cash and equivalent investments

Savings accounts and similar 'cash' investments, while safe and liquid, lack growth potential.

Cash can be more than money in the bank

Investing is using your money to make more money. The kind of cash kept in your pocket or in your bank account isn't normally thought of as an investment. It's savings. But you first have to accumulate cash before you have enough to invest, and some places are better than others for getting you started on the road to financial security.

The most common savings vehicles include bank savings accounts, short-term guaranteed investment certificates, money market accounts, Canada Savings Bonds and treasury bills.

Savings accounts

These are a good place to park your money for a very short time while you save for a specific purpose such as an appliance or a more permanent investment, but paying the bank for the privilege of using your money doesn't make much sense. Typically, a savings account will pay you a rate of interest significantly below the rate of inflation. For the past few years the interest rate paid on savings accounts has been below 1%, while inflation has averaged 1.3%.

Debt instruments: Governments or companies sell debt instruments when they need to borrow large amounts from investors.

Money market accounts

Money market accounts pay a much better rate of interest than savings accounts — typically one or two percentage points above the inflation rate. They may be a much better place to store larger amounts of savings, and are quite secure

Historical performance of cash investments

Cash and cash equivalent investments have traditionally
had the lowest rates of return of all types of investments.
The chart shows how $100 would have grown over a
recent 15-year period if you'd invested in 5-year GICs,
90-day T-bills and Canada Savings Bonds

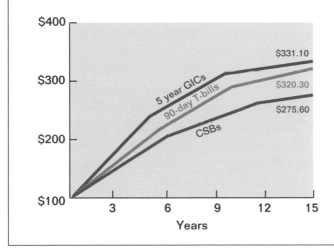

because they generally invest in high-grade, short-term
government and corporate debt.

Treasury bills (T-bills)

The federal and provincial governments sell these debt
obligations for terms of three, six or 12 months.
Technically, they don't pay interest but instead are
bought at a discount to their value at maturity. For
instance, a three-month T-bill with a maturity value of
$100 might be bought for $98.50. Over three months,
your gain equals an annual interest rate of 6.09%. If

you sell a T-bill before the maturity date, though, you'll receive only what another investor is willing to pay for it that day.

Traditionally sold in large denominations, T-bills have always appealed to big institutions such as banks and insurance companies, as well as a few very wealthy investors. The reason is that they are a safe and liquid place to park extra cash while earning an interest rate that equals or exceeds inflation. Brokers have made pieces of T-bills available to retail investors for amounts as small as $1,000.

Guaranteed investment certificates (GICs)

GICs are generally one to five-year deposits with a bank or other financial institution like a trust company. You agree to keep the money in the GIC for a set period in return for a set rate of interest.

Compound interest GICs pay you interest on your interest. Instead of paying the interest to you outside the GIC, the interest is added to your original deposit and subsequent interest payments are based on this larger new amount.

GICs are relatively safe investments. However, it's important to consider the chances that you'll need to access your money before the GIC matures. If this happens, you'll likely lose some of your accumulated interest. In fact, some GICs can't be cashed before the term is up.

There's also a risk if you put your money in a five-year GIC and interest rates go up. If this happens, you may have missed a chance to invest your money at a higher rate.

Canada Savings Bonds (CSBs)

Since CSBs first went on sale in 1946 they have
become an important source of funds for the federal
government. CSBs come in many variations and are
often available through payroll deduction.

There are three main types of CSBs: regular
interest, compound interest and RRSP bonds. You can
buy a CSB with as little as $100, and most series can
be cashed at any time. Until the late 1990s, CSBs were
sold only once a year, usually between mid-
October and November 1. In 1998, the
government made some changes. CSBs could be
bought over a period of six months, with a
different series available each month.

It's wise to remember that while CSBs are a
reasonable way to amass short-term savings,
they aren't an effective way to grow the value of your
investment portfolio. Neither, of course, are bank
savings accounts, treasury bills or GICs. While each
investment vehicle we discussed can appear to
increase in value over time, none can offer a rate of
return significantly above inflation. As such, they will
never put you in a position to fulfil your wealth-
building strategies. To do this, you need to take a bit
more risk with your money, either as a lender or as an
owner. The following chapters on fixed-income
securities, equity investments and mutual funds
describe some of the investment vehicles that can help
you do just that.

Payroll deduction:
Automatic
deduction before
tax from your
salary that is
invested by your
employer in
CSBs.

Chapter 11

Fixed-income investments

When you want stability and steady income in your portfolio, fixed-income investments like bonds are the answer.

Understanding bonds

Bonds offer a lot to investors of every age group and background. They pay you interest regularly and can also have a stabilizing effect on your portfolio.

Governments and companies that need to raise large amounts of money issue bonds. Each bond has a face value that represents the original amount the issuer borrowed. The bond's face value, also called par value, is usually only paid back at the end of the bond's term, which can be up to 30 years. In the meantime, the bond pays interest — the payment is known as the coupon — based on its face value. If a bond with a par value of $1,000 pays 8% interest, then you will get $80 in interest per year.

Par:
What a bond will be worth when it matures, also called its face value.

Coupon:
A bond's annual interest rate based on its par value.

Yield to maturity:
The return you'll get on your investment if you hold the bond until it matures.

Most often, you won't buy bonds directly from the issuer, but through an investment dealer on the bond market. How much you pay will often either be higher or lower than the bond's face value, depending on how competitive the bond's coupon is compared with interest rates on other investments. The price you actually pay on a bond will affect your return, or what's called your "yield to maturity."

You might pay $900 for a 30-year bond with a face value of $1,000 and a coupon of 8%. When the bond matures, you will get the full $1,000 face value, giving you a $100 profit to add to the 8% interest you get each year. That means your yield to maturity over the 30 years is roughly 9.26% and not 8%.

Bond prices mainly fluctuate whenever there are concrete or anticipated changes in general market interest rates. When interest rates rise, bond prices drop, and when they fall, bond prices rise. These price changes keep bond returns in line with the current level of interest rates. The best strategy for most people is to buy bonds for their income and for the stability they can bring to a portfolio. If general interest rates fall and the price of your bond rises, you might consider selling and treat any profit as a windfall.

Not all bonds are created equal

As you might expect, the safety level of bonds varies a lot, based on the borrower's ability to repay your money. Large, well-established companies with a track record of paying off their debts generally are considered safe investments, as are the Canadian federal and provincial governments with their unique ability to rely upon current and, if necessary, unborn taxpayers to raise money. On the other hand, smaller companies, especially those without a proven track record of performance, will have to pay higher rates of interest to compensate you for the extra risk you'd take buying their bonds.

Types of bonds

There are many different types of bonds, and some of these have special privileges or features to make them more attractive to investors. Since the purpose of this section of the book is to give an overview of investments, we'll limit our discussion to bond types.

Federal government bonds, known as *Canadas*, pay a relatively low rate of interest because they are backed by the government's power to tax its citizens, which makes them one of the safest investments available.

All provincial governments in Canada also issue bonds, to fund spending programs and service their accumulated debts. The interest rates payable on provincial bonds are usually slightly higher than those paid on similar federal bonds, and rates will vary depending on each province's credit rating.

Corporations also issue bonds and they're either *secured* or *unsecured*. Secured bonds are backed by specific company assets that bondholders can seize and sell if the company defaults on its payments. Unsecured bonds, otherwise known as debentures, are backed only by the general creditworthiness of the company that issued them. Although less safe than government bonds, top-rated corporate bonds are considered secure and will generally pay a higher yield than similar government bonds.

Preferred shares

Preferred shares are actually equities since they represent ownership in a company. But because preferred shares usually offer a fixed payment called a dividend, they are considered fixed-income securities. However, dividends are not a legal requirement like interest payments on bonds. If the company's directors decide to skip the payment of a preferred dividend there is little the preferred shareholder can do about it. Normally, however, no dividends can be paid to common shareholders until the preferred shareholders

Historical performance of long, short and mid-term bonds

Longer term bonds tend to outperform other bonds over the long haul, but they're more volatile over the short-term. The chart shows the performance of long, medium and short-term bonds over a recent 15-year period.

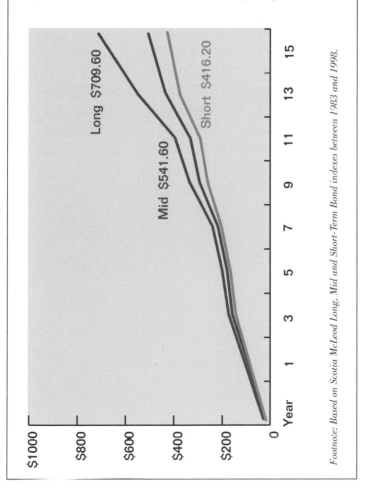

Footnote: Based on Scotia McLeod Long, Mid and Short-Term Bond indexes between 1983 and 1998.

have received all the dividends to which they're entitled.

While preferred shares don't offer the same potential for capital appreciation as common shares, they usually pay a much higher dividend that doesn't fluctuate. For these reasons, preferred shares are very attractive to conservative, income-oriented investors.

Lighter tax treatment of dividends
Another attraction is that the dividend income from preferred and other shares often qualifies for generous tax treatment. Depending on your income level, tax on dividends is often less than for other kinds of investment income. You'll find details about dividend taxes later in this book.

Chapter 12

Equity investments

In the spirit of a marathon runner, equities out perform all other asset classes in the long haul.

Patience, good judgement can reap superior returns

Equities or stocks have traditionally delivered the highest returns of the three asset classes over the long-term, with emphasis on long-term. For most of us, the best strategy for investing in stocks means being patient and careful, and putting most of the money earmarked for equities into the stocks of large, profitable companies with solid track records.

When you buy stock in a company you are buying a share of the business. You are a part-owner with the right to vote in the company's affairs and the right to share in any profits. That's why it's crucial to invest in a profitable company, one that brings in more money than it pays out.

Since many forces can hurt a company's profitability, buying shares is usually riskier than investing in bonds or cash-equivalent investments. Share prices can rise and fall from one day to the next, and even during the course of a single day's trading. But over time this one-step-back, two-steps-forward action evens out into a rising trend.

When a company earns healthy profits, it may share the wealth by paying you dividends on the shares you own. However, a company isn't obliged to do so. As well, companies must first make interest payments to their bondholders, plus pay dividends to preferred shareholders, before any common stock dividends can be declared.

Companies that don't pay dividends generally are riskier investments. For most of us, prudent stock investing means buying shares of large, well-known and profitable companies that pay a good percentage of their profits in dividends, and then holding these stocks for 10 years or more. The only exceptions to holding a stock for the long-term would be if the company no longer seemed a good investment, or if you had achieved your target return and see better investment opportunities elsewhere.

Types of shares

Industry insiders use a variety of terms to describe stocks that share similar characteristics. The three most common ones are blue chip, junior and penny.

The term *blue chip* is used for big companies that pay dividends and consistently increase profits in good times and bad. They usually are the dominant players in their industry, and have a lot of earning power and top management. Shares that would fall in this category include many of the banks and companies like Bell Canada, Coca Cola, IBM and General Motors.

Junior stocks are common shares of smaller companies that lack significant profits, market dominance and a track record for earnings. Small companies in emerging industries such as technology are typically considered juniors. *Penny stocks* are generally considered very risky and are often associated with companies exploring for oil and gas, precious metals or base metals. These stocks trade for less than $1, mainly on the Alberta and Vancouver stock

Blue chip:
Large companies that pay dividends and consistently increase profits, regardless of economic conditions.

Junior stocks:
Shares of smaller companies with a limited history of earnings, often in emerging industries like technology.

Penny stocks:
Shares of companies that are very risky, often exploring for oil and gas or precious metals. Trade for less than $1.

Over-the-counter market:
A securities market made up of dealers who make trades by phone or computer. Also called "unlisted," "street," "between," or "inter-dealer" market.

exchanges or on *over-the-counter* markets. Most people should never have more than a small portion of their portfolio invested in junior or penny stocks.

How the market values stock

The main influence on stock prices is supply and demand. Prices move up when more investors want to buy a stock than sell it, and they move down when more investors want to sell than buy the stock.

A growing economy and low interest rates generally have a positive effect on the stock market. Many other factors affect the price of an individual stock, including the company's past performance, its prospects and strategies for growth, and the health of the sector in which it operates. For most investors, the best strategy for stock market investing is the tried and true buy-and-hold approach. This means you buy well-run companies with a proven record of earnings and bright growth prospects, and keep them for the long-term despite the ups and downs of the overall stock market.

Chapter 13

Mutual funds

Relative newcomers to the investment marketplace, mutual funds offer investors many benefits.

Why invest in mutual funds

For increasing numbers of Canadians, mutual funds are one of the easiest and most effective ways to gain entry into the mysterious world of stocks and bonds. In its simplest terms, a mutual fund is a pool of money that is managed by professional portfolio managers to match particular investment objectives.

This money is gathered by the fund sponsor — perhaps a bank, mutual fund company or life insurance firm — through the sale of shares or units to investors. The money, called the assets under management, is invested in a broad range of securities or commodities. The fund's return depends on the performance of the investments made by the manager, and the return is usually made up of a combination of capital gains, dividends and interest.

Diversification: *The principle of holding many types of securities or commodities, to reduce overall risk.*

Today's investors can choose between funds that invest in T-bills, bonds, mortgages, real estate, blue-chip companies, precious metals and everything in between — in both the domestic and international markets. Despite the diversity, however, the underlying advantages generally are the same for all funds:

- professional management;

- *diversification* among many different securities or commodities, thus reducing the effect of a gain or loss on any one investment; and

- the convenience of being able to make small lump-sum purchases, or automatic monthly purchases from your bank account.

As the accompanying table shows, investing regularly in mutual funds — as with stocks — can reduce your cost per unit. And when the unit price is lower, your money gives you more units of the fund.

How dollar-cost averaging lowers your cost per share

Investor A Buys $750 worth of ABC mutual fund each month for 6 months

Month	1	2	3	4	5	6	TOTALS	
ABC unit price	$10	$7.85	$11.50	$9.90	$13	$8.50		= $9.83
Units bought	75	95	65	75	57	88	455 units	per unit
Cost	$750	$745.75	$747.50	$742.50	$741	$748	$4,474.75	

Investor B Buys $4,500 worth of ABCmutual fund in month 1

Month	1	2	3	4	5	6	TOTALS	
ABC unit price	$10	-		-	-	-		= $10.00
Units bought	450	-	-	-	-	-	450 units	per unit
Cost	$4,500	-	-	-	-	-	$4,500	

Mutual fund fees

When you buy units in a mutual fund you may be charged a commission, also known as a load. If you're charged such a commission it will usually be a *front-end or back-end* load. A few funds charge both a front-end and back-end load. There are also *no-load* funds, and these are sold by most banks, trust companies and some independent fund companies. Whatever type of fund you buy, you also pay management fees, but you may not even notice. Management fees are deducted from the fund before the fund states its returns. These fees cover the cost of operating the fund.

Don't, however, become fixated on fees and

Front-end load:
The money some funds charge when you buy units.

Back-end load:
The money some funds charge when you sell your units.

No-load:
You are not charged to buy or redeem units in this type of fund.

expenses. Cheaper funds are not necessarily better funds. While fees do have an impact on your return, they are only one component of good fund selection. Where two funds are fairly equal in most respects, the cheaper fund is likely your better option.

How to analyze mutual fund performance

The obvious key measure of a mutual fund's performance is how much of a return you earn investing in it. Fund companies are prone to trumpeting superior returns on some funds, while glossing over poor-performing funds.

Not surprisingly, many people tend to invest in funds that have experienced exceptional returns in the past year. This can be a mistake if the fund has shown volatile returns over time. As the standard disclaimer says, "Past performance is no guarantee of future performance."

Beyond a fund's annual returns, there are other ways to measure fund performance. One important issue to assess is how risky your fund is. A way of doing this is to look at how volatile a fund is, that is how much its unit price moves up and down. The more it fluctuates, the riskier it is. To check your fund's volatility, look up your fund regularly in the financial pages of main Canadian newspapers. To get a longer term perspective, read over the material your fund company sends.

Choose funds that fit your goals

With over 2,000 mutual funds to choose from, you can't complain about a lack of variety. If anything, there's almost too much choice in the mutual fund market today. However, if you keep your personal investment objectives in mind, then your search for the right fund should be quite easy. Although the industry uses over 30 formal classifications, most funds fit into one of the following broad categories.

Money market funds

These invest in government T-bills and short-term corporate borrowings. As such, they're suitable for short-term investment. These funds' returns are quite low, but stable over time. Two types are available, Canadian money market funds and international money market funds. Fees for money market funds are generally the lowest of all fund types.

Bond funds

These invest in government and company bonds and generally aim to provide regular interest payments to their unit holders. Most bond funds offer fairly stable returns over time. However, some that invest in longer-term or lower quality bonds of emerging market countries can be quite volatile. You will also find short-term bond funds that offer lower, more reliable returns. International bond funds let you invest outside of Canada to take advantage of higher interest rates elsewhere. Fees for Canadian bond funds are quite modest, while those for international funds can be relatively high.

Balanced funds

These funds hold a mix of stocks, bonds and money market investments. They are meant to be a replacement for building your own portfolio. Instead of buying money market, bond and equity funds to have a balanced portfolio, you can achieve the same result investing in a single balanced fund. However, most balanced funds are managed to meet the needs of conservative investors, which might not necessarily fit your profile. Fees for balanced funds tend to be relatively high

Equity funds

There's a wide range of equity or stock funds. They range from relatively low risk dividend funds that invest in blue chips and preferred shares to high risk funds that buy only stocks in small mining exploration companies. Index funds aim to emulate the returns of well-known local and international stock market indexes like the TSE 300 Composite Index. You will also find many international equity funds, from those that invest in all major economic regions to some that invest in only emerging market countries. All equity funds aim to deliver superior performance over the long-term. Fees for equity funds vary depending on the type of fund. Index funds often have the lowest fee structure, while international and specialty funds generally have the highest.

Chapter 14

How to balance risk & return

Every investment decision you make must weigh potential return against degree of risk.

Investing is a balancing act

Now that you understand the basic features of many investments, which ones will you choose? All of us have to face this question. And while there are general guidelines on what to do, selecting investments remains an imprecise science. You cannot be sure exactly how your decisions will pan out.

However, every investor's goal should be to buy investments that fit their objectives, and which will get them where they're going with the minimum of risk. It's a delicate balancing act. You have to strike a happy medium between the return you want and the likelihood of each investment achieving that return.

Don't think of risk only as the possibility that you'll lose your money. Often risk is subtler than that. It can be something less drastic, such as missing your goal by a percent or two. In fact, you can take too much or not enough risk in investing. The key is to navigate a path between the two extremes. Both risk types — too little or not enough — are equally perilous.

Why playing it safe can be the riskiest strategy of all

In certain circumstances, secure investments such as short-term deposits and T-bills are fraught with danger. This occurs when they are improperly used as long-term investments, such as a 40-year-old saving for retirement 25 years away. The risk stems from inflation, the number one enemy for anyone trying to grow their money. Inflation pushes up prices, which means a dollar today will buy you less in the future.

The worst case scenario is when the inflation rate is higher than the interest rate your investments are paying. If this happens, your investment will lose part of its buying power. You will be going broke safely. The chart shows how a dollar today declines in value over 30 years when inflation is 3%. To maintain your dollar's buying power in this example, it must grow by at least 3% per year. Any return higher than 3% will actually start to increase your buying power.

When you have a long time available before you will need your money — say 10 years or more — then you

Declining dollar

After 30 years, one dollar today will buy you only 40 cents worth of goods if inflation averages 3% per year. That's why it's essential if you want to grow your wealth to earn a return on your investment that outstrips inflation.

| 1 yr – $0.97 | 5 yrs – $0.86 | 10 yrs – $0.74 |

| 15 yrs – $0.64 | 20 yrs – $0.54 | 25 yrs – $0.47 | 30 yrs – $0.40 |

The link between risk and return

safest

| Government treasury bills | GICs | Government bonds | Corporate bonds |

can afford to take on additional risk. Time reduces the higher risks inherent in such investments as stocks. Over the short-term, stock prices can fluctuate wildly. But over time they tend to grow faster than inflation.

Beware of taking too much risk

While having time on your side puts you in a position to take on more risk, it doesn't necessarily follow that this is the best strategy for everyone. What you need always to evaluate is whether in fact you need to take on increased risk. If a safer strategy will get you to your goals, then it makes more sense to be conservative. Taking on higher risk could mean missing an important goal that is otherwise easily within your grasp, or worse still, cause you to lose money you simply can't afford to be without.

The world's richest man, Bill Gates of software giant Microsoft, doesn't need to take any risks with his billions. In fact, his biggest challenge is to reduce his risk. Right now he has most of his money tied up in the software giant, which is like having all his eggs in one

| | | | **riskiest** |
| Preferred shares | Blue-chip common shares | Penny stocks | Futures |

basket. So his strategy is to scale back his ownership of Microsoft and buy safer T-bills. A nice problem to have, but the point is that you, too, may have no reason to increase your risk exposure.

Another important input into the risk-return equation is emotional rather than financial. Your feelings towards risk are crucial to successful investing. While we all would like to think of ourselves as efficient, unemotional money managers, the reality is that we're not. Most of us worry at least a little when our investments take a steep, albeit temporary, dive on the downside. For some of us, this worry can turn to panic, prompting us to sell at the worst possible moment.

Don't kid yourself when it comes to how much risk you think you can handle. Remember that the stock market is known for going through periods of extreme volatility, at times losing 20% to 25% of its value in a single day. If such a steep tumble is going to leave you queasy, then hold back a little on your diet of stocks.

Futures:
A saleable agreement to buy or sell a commodity or financial product in the future at a set price.

Understand the link between risk and return

A useful tool for understanding the risk profile of different investments in the risk-return spectrum (see chart on pages 110-111). It gives you a snapshot of various investments arranged from the safest on the left to the riskiest on the right. The safest investments, government T-bills, also offer the lowest potential return, while the riskiest investments, futures contracts, provide an opportunity to make a lot of money, but with extreme perils.

What this tells you is that there is a trade-off to be made between risk and return. The higher the return you want from your investments, the more risk you will likely need to take. Of course, the opposite is also true. If you only need a small return on your money, then the investments to the left of the spectrum will suffice.

When looking at the risk-return spectrum, also consider the amount of time you have available to invest. If your goal is only a short while away — two years or less — then keep to the left of the spectrum. The longer your time horizon, the more freedom you have to move to the right of the spectrum.

Know what risks could strike your investments

Like most people, you probably think of risk as the chance that the value of your investment will drop, or that you'll get a smaller return than you were counting on. But when it comes to deciding how to invest your hard-earned savings, it pays to take a closer look at the specific types of risk that could upset your dreams. The major risk types are interest rate risk, inflation risk, market risk and default risk.

Interest rate risk

When interest rates rise, the value of most investments goes down. The reasons are complex, but basically higher interest rates make existing securities unattractive compared to new investments that pay more interest. Fixed-income investments are particularly sensitive to interest rate changes, although equities are affected to a lesser extent. Between fixed-income investments, longer-term investments are more vulnerable than short-term ones. This is because people who own short-term investments have less time to wait to reinvest their money at the new higher interest rates.

Inflation or buying power risk

Rising inflation is a major risk for all investments, although the biggest impact is on fixed-income and cash investments. People with fixed-income investments face the risk that the inflation rate will be more than their rate of return. If this happens, then your money's buying power shrinks making your poorer than when you started.

Market risk

Stocks are especially vulnerable to the natural ups and downs of the market. An extreme example of market risk is when stock markets crash. In October 1987, stock markets around the world plummeted up to 30%. No one knows exactly why stock markets crash, save for the fact that there are many times more sellers in the market than buyers, which forces prices sharply down. Fortunately, markets often recover quickly from such drastic episodes. In fact, within two years of the 1987 debacle, most markets had regained their former ground.

Less extreme than crashes are declines over a period of time called bear markets. These occur quite regularly and typically last a few months to 18 months. They affect almost all stocks, regardless of how well the particular companies are doing. Since the purpose of stocks is long-term growth, people who use stocks properly can typically afford to wait out market declines.

Bear market:
A market where most prices are declining; usually happens during economic recessions.

Default risk

Also called business risk, this the chance that a company or a government will find itself in severe financial trouble. If you own the issuer's bonds or stocks, their value could plunge substantially if investors fear the company will default on paying interest or principal. In the worst case, a company may have to declare bankruptcy, which could result in creditors and shareholders losing their full investment. Shareholders, however, are particularly vulnerable since they are the last to be paid from what remains of the company's assets.

What you can do about risk

Two ways exist to reduce risk in investing. The first — and most important — is *asset allocation*; dividing your money between the three asset classes of cash, fixed-income and equity. The rule of thumb is that your equity exposure should be the result of 100 minus your age. So if you're 40, then 60% of your portfolio might be in equities. The other general rule is that most working people won't need to keep more than 10% of their money in cash investments. Of course, these general parameters won't apply to everyone. Research shows that up to 90% of your portfolio's long-term performance can be traced back to your asset allocation, so spend some time to get it right.

Business cycle: *The economy's natural ebb and flow through serial stages of recession and recovery.*

The second way to reduce risk is to diversify your individual investments across industry sectors, by country, and by time. The first two are quite self-explanatory. Since companies in different industries do better at different stages of the *business cycle*, it makes sense to diversify across industry types to temper reliance on any one sector. Investing internationally also reduces your risk since you are not so heavily reliant on home markets for your returns.

Asset allocation: *Strategically dividing your investments between the three asset classes to fit your objectives, return expectations and risk tolerance.*

The third type of diversification, time diversification, deserves a more detailed explanation because it's often overlooked. In the early 1980s, many people were drawn to GICs because they paid double-digit interest. Much to their dismay, however, inflation continued to rage in the next few years, eventually exceeding the rate of return on those investments. Had these people diversified their GICs by time — i.e. spread their money evenly between one, three, and 5-year terms — inflation's impact would have been less dramatic.

The thinking goes something like this: When the

one-year GIC matures, you can renew for five years at the new higher rates. Two years later when the original three-year GIC comes due, you can renew at the new prevailing five-year rates, and likewise two years later when the five-year certificate is up. All the time part of your money is being reinvested at the prevailing rates, thereby reducing your risk of being outpaced by inflation. You can do the same thing — called "laddering" — with bonds of different terms.

Chapter 15

Tax planning for families

By understanding the tax system you can pay less tax and keep more to invest.

How the tax system works

Canada imposes a graduated income tax system on all residents, and this system comprises three tax brackets. The thinking behind the brackets is that the more you earn, the greater your ability to help the federal and provincial governments finance the operation of the country. Basically, the more you earn, the higher the percentage of tax you pay. Here's how it works:

Income	Tax rate*
up to $29,590...	26%
$29,590 to $59,180..................................	39%
$49,180..	44%

* A combination of federal and provincial tax rates.

For most Canadians, the rate of tax paid is a blended rate that varies with income. For example, somebody earning $65,000 a year would pay 26% tax on the first $29,590 in earnings, plus 39% on the next $29,590, and 44% on the balance of $2,380.40. This figure equals a blended or average tax rate of 33.25%, as follows:

26% on the first $29,590	= $ 7,693.40
39% on the next $29,590	= $11,540.10
44% on amount above $59,590	= $ 2,380.40
	$21,613.90

$21,613.90 is **33.25%** of $65,000.

Marginal versus average tax rate

When it comes to smart tax planning, however, you have to keep in mind the difference between your average and your marginal tax rates. While your average tax rate is the percentage of tax you pay on your total income, your marginal rate is the amount of tax you pay for the last dollar earned. As a result, anything you can do to reduce your taxable income has a far greater effect than you might expect. Using the above example, an RRSP contribution of $5,000 would serve to lower taxable income to $60,000 from $65,000. If the average tax rate applied, the taxpayer could expect to save $1,662.50 — 33.25% of $5,000. However, because income tax is applied in brackets, the $5,000 RRSP contribution will be used to offset the last $5,000 of income earned, all of which would have been subject to the highest marginal tax rate: 44%. As a result, the actual tax savings is $2,200 — 44% of $5,000. In fact, because of the surtaxes applied by the federal and provincial governments, the marginal rate would probably be about 50% and the savings would be even greater.

Marginal tax rate:
The amount of tax you pay on the last dollar you earn.

Average tax rate:
The percentage of tax you pay on your total income.

How your taxes are calculated

While every individual tax return is different, completing all income tax returns involves calculating four basic components: total income, deductions, taxable income and tax credits. After you've calculated your total income, you then subtract your various

Surtax:
A "temporary" tax on tax usually charged to those in the highest marginal tax bracket.

119

deductions to reach your taxable income. From your taxable income, you then subtract various tax-credits. Over the next few pages, we look in detail at what goes into each step.

Total income has four sources

The federal government considers four types of income taxable and each is treated differently under Canadian tax laws.

Income from employment

Employment income is taxed on a gross-receipt basis. This means that, unlike a business, you can't deduct all the costs incurred to earn a living. However, you may deduct a few employment-related expenses such as pension contributions, union dues and child care expenses. Employment income is subject to the graduated income tax scale we just looked at.

Income from business

Business income is the profit earned from producing and selling goods or services. It's taxed on a net income basis, which is calculated by using generally accepted accounting principals or GAAP. To encourage the growth of small business in Canada, smaller companies are eligible for a small business deduction which can reduce their overall tax rate.

Income from property

Owners can deduct reasonable expenses such as property taxes, repairs, maintenance and, in some cases, financing costs to acquire the income property. Only net income in subject to tax.

Capital gains and losses

Both individual taxpayers and corporations must pay
tax on capital gains. A capital gain results when you
sell a capital property or investment for more than you
paid. A capital loss occurs when you sell some-thing
for less than you paid. If you lose money on your
investment, you can use it to offset the amount of tax
payable on investments that rose in value.

What you can deduct
from total income

The next step in calculating your income tax is to make
use of all available deductions from total income.
Here's a few of the most common ones.

RRSP contributions

For most Canadians, especially those without an
employer-sponsored pension plan, this is the biggest
and best deduction going. Anyone who has earned
income and is less than 69 years old is eligible. The
maximum deduction is 18% of earned income up to
$13,500 a year, less the value of contributions
to any other registered plan.

Tax deduction:
An expense that
reduces your
total income that
can be taxed.

Pension plan contributions

Any contributions you make to any employer-
sponsored pension plan are also tax-deductible.

Carrying charges and interest expenses

Essentially, these are expenses incurred in your
investment activities. They include things like interest
paid on money borrowed to earn investment income,

and various fees like management and custodial fees, except for the annual administration fee on self-directed RRSPs. Interest paid on money borrowed to make an RRSP investment is not a deductible expense. You can deduct the annual cost of your safety deposit box.

Business losses
If you are employed but also operate your own business, you can use losses in your business to offset your employment income. If you are receiving rent on a house that doesn't cover the interest on the mortgage plus other property expenses, you incur a loss that can be used to offset your employment income.

Child care expenses
You can deduct up to $7,000 for each child up to age seven, and up to $4,000 for each child aged seven to 16. Generally, child care expenses are eligible only if they are incurred to enable you to work, attend school or do research, and if they are fully documented. If you are married, or have been in a common-law relationship, the spouse with the lower income can deduct child care expenses.

Alimony
Any alimony payments made due to a court order or written separation agreement are deductible from your income.

Other deductions
Other eligible deductions include union or professional association dues and moving expenses incurred to

secure employment, provided you are at least 40 kilometers closer to work.

Taxable income

Once you subtract all your eligible deductions from total income, you arrive at what the government considers to be your taxable income. Thus, the next step in determining your income tax bill is a matter of multiplying your taxable income by the appropriate tax brackets we discussed earlier. However, you aren't finished yet. Most taxpayers can further reduce their tax bill by applying various tax credits.

Taxable income:
Your total yearly earnings after deductions used as the amount on which you calculate the taxes you must pay.

Tax credits

The final step in calculating your tax bill — or refund — is to determine the value of your tax credits. The largest single tax credit for most people is their basic personal exemption.

There are many other tax credits and they apply to a wide range of eligible expenses including medical bills, charitable donations and political contributions. In addition, taxpayers over the age of 65 can claim special age tax credits if they care for disabled family members. For investors, there is also a dividend tax credit which can effectively lower the rate of tax you pay on dividends compared to other forms of income. We'll have more to say on this later.

Minimizing your taxes

With some simple forethought you can reduce your taxes without breaking the law.

Focus on tax-favoured income

When it comes to minimizing your tax bill, some types of income are better than others. Knowing this ahead of time lets you emphasize the types of income that will leave more in your pocket after tax.

Your home is a tax shelter

One of the best ways to minimize your personal tax is to pay no tax at all. Owning your home is primarily a lifestyle consideration and it shouldn't be looked upon strictly as an investment. For most people, however, the principal residence is also one of the cornerstones of a sound financial planning strategy. One of the main reasons is that any gain in the value of your home, no matter how large, is completely tax-free.

Put money in dividend-paying investments

While income from employment and interest income from investments are simply taxed at your marginal tax rate, dividend income from taxable Canadian corporations receives preferential treatment that can save you tax dollars.

Why do dividends get special treatment? Dividends represent your share of a company's after-tax profits. Since income tax has already been paid on dividends at the corporate level, it would be unfair to tax them again in your hands. However, rather than make dividends completely tax-free, the government has devised the dividend tax credit, and it may give you substantial tax relief.

As peculiar as it seems, here's how it works. You receive an annual dividend from ABC Company Ltd. of

$1,000. To calculate the dividend tax credit, you gross up this amount by 25%. Thus, your $1,000 of dividend income becomes $1,250. And this amount is taxed at your marginal rate.

If paying your marginal tax rate on more income than you actually received hardly sounds like tax relief, don't worry. Here's where the tax credit comes in. The next step is to reduce the amount of tax owing by your tax credit. In this case, you would claim a credit of $166.63 — 13.33% on this grossed-up amount of $1,250.

The example below shows how the dividend tax credit works, assuming a marginal federal tax rate of 29%:

Dividend received	$1,000.00
Grossed-up amount	$1,250.00
Federal tax at 29%	$ 362.50
Dividend tax credit	
13.33% x grossed-up amount	$ 166.63
Net federal tax (federal tax minus the dividend tax credit)	$ 195.87
Provincial tax at 50% of net federal tax	$ 97.94
Total tax payable on dividend ($195.87 + $97.94):	**$ 293.81**

In this example, the tax payable on dividend income is $293.81 or just more than 29%. In contrast,

tax on equivalent employment or interest income would
be $435 or 43.5% (based on a marginal federal tax rate
of 29% plus an average provincial rate of 14.5%).

Capital gains are taxed less than interest

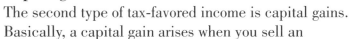

The second type of tax-favored income is capital gains.
Basically, a capital gain arises when you sell an
investment, such as a stock, bond or real estate,
for more than you paid for it. The bad news is
that you have to pay tax on your gain. The good
news is that the rate of tax on capital gains —
as in the case of dividends — is lower than the
rate for employment or interest income.

Adjusted cost base:
The price you
paid for an asset
plus expenses
you incurred
buying it, such as
commission.

Basically, the tax-favored status of capital
gains is achieved by treating only 75% of the gain as
taxable. Here's how it works. You buy 100 common
shares of ABC Company Ltd. at $6 and sell them two
years later for $10 a share. In the year they are sold,
your tax liability would be calculated as follows:

Gross proceeds from sale:	$1,000.00
less: adjusted cost base – cost of shares ($600) + commission ($17)	$617.00
	$383.00
Less: commission on sale	$25.00
Capital gain	$358.00
Taxable capital gain (75% of $358)	**$268.50**

Again, an investor with a combined provincial and
federal marginal tax rate of 43.5% would pay $116.80

in tax on the taxable gain of $268.50. However, the
$116.50 represents a tax rate of 33%. If the $358 were
employment or interest income, and not a capital gain,
you would be subject to $155.73 — or $39.23 more —
in tax.

Consider income splitting strategies

Another potentially effective way to reduce your tax is
to transfer as much income or income-producing assets
as possible to a family member with little or no income
and a comparatively lower tax rate.

*Income splitting:
Moving taxable
income from a
high tax-bracket
person to one in
a lower bracket
to cut your
overall tax bill.*

Before you start giving things away to
lessen your tax load, however, you need to know
about Revenue Canada's attribution rules.
Basically, they're designed to ensure that you
won't give, or pretend to give, your assets to
family members for the purpose of avoiding tax.
Selling assets to family members is fine. But if you try
to give things away, or sell them for less than full
market value, the attribution rules come into play, and
the full tax consequences are passed back to you. The
only exception to the attribution rules occurs in a
marital breakup. Despite these limitations, you have
several legal ways to effectively split your income to
minimize tax.

Carefully choose who pays for expenses

In some marriages, the lower-income earner gets stuck
with the grocery bills while the high-income earner
handles the high finance. This is not always the best
approach. The higher income spouse should first pay
all personal family expenses while the lower income
spouse invests as much of his or her income as

129

practical. Thus, the spouse with the lower income pays less tax on the investment income, and the value of the investment can grow faster. This approach will also reduce the family's overall tax burden.

Another useful strategy is for the higher-income spouse to maximize contributions to their personal and spousal RRSPs. This person pays the highest marginal tax rate and thus qualifies for the bigger tax refund.

Start a spousal RRSP

This brings us to perhaps the best income-splitting strategy of all: the spousal RRSP. If contributing to the highest-income earner's RRSP produces the biggest tax refund but is creating an imbalance between your ultimate retirement incomes, the spousal RRSP can provide help. Basically, it allows you to contribute up to your annual RRSP limit into your spouse's RRSP and deduct the full amount of the contribution from your taxable income. If you pay tax at a higher rate than your spouse, you come out farther ahead than if your spouse makes the same contribution. You'll read more about spousal RRSPs in chapter 20.

Spousal RRSP: An RRSP in a lower-income spouse's name, but to which a higher income spouse contributes to reduce combined taxes at withdrawal.

Give money to the lower-income spouse

In most two-income families, money flows pretty freely back and forth and it's difficult to say who came up with the money for last week's groceries or who earned the money for the CSBs. But it's a different situation when one spouse earns considerably more than the other. Revenue Canada tends to notice when the low-income spouse, for example, makes an investment that is greater than his or her annual income, and is ready to apply the attribution rules. If they do, there are a few ways to minimize the impact.

If you give your spouse money to invest, you have to pay tax on the income earned by the investment, but you don't have to pay tax on the interest earned on the income. Let's say you give your spouse $10,000 to invest in CSBs at 5% interest. At tax time, you will have to declare $500 in interest. However, any subsequent income earned by the $500 that is reinvested will be attributed to your spouse's income.

You could also lend $10,000 to your spouse. As long as you charge reasonable interest — the government publishes the "prescribed" interest rate each year — and pay tax on it, the income earned on the investment will be attributed to your spouse. In this case, the investment will be worthwhile only if its return is greater than the rate of interest and taxes on the loan.

Hire your family

If you own a business, hiring your spouse or children to provide support services can provide several benefits. Obviously, it gives your spouse and children gainful employment that boosts family income. But it also allows you to split the family's overall income between several family members and reduce the overall tax burden. And in the case of your spouse, it allows you to contribute to CPP/QPP and other deferred-income plans such as an RRSP.

Borrow to invest and deduct the interest

If you borrow money to invest, Revenue Canada allows you to deduct the cost of borrowing from your taxable income.

131

If you want to make your total debt load as tax-efficient as possible, keep this special treatment for investments in mind. You might plan to buy a new car and invest in stocks at about the same time, yet only have enough cash to cover one or the other. Because interest paid on borrowings for investments is tax-deductible, you should pay cash for the car and finance the stock purchase. By the same token, if you can repay a debt early, always put your money towards the debt with the least tax benefits, in this case, the car.

One final word on this subject: always keep immaculate records of your personal and investment borrowings. If you use your line of credit to fund household purchases and investments, it will be difficult to tell how much of your interest payments are attributable to a specific investment. You might want to set up a separate line of credit for your investments to simplify your record-keeping.

Chapter 17

Defer tax to a later date

While it may sound odd, the government has plans that help you reduce your taxes and save for retirement.

Make Revenue Canada wait

Whoever said "never put off to tomorrow what you can do today" certainly wasn't thinking about income tax. When it comes to paying income tax, sooner is definitely worse than later. Deferring tax gives you more money now which, if wisely invested, can generate a far greater amount of wealth for you than by using after-tax dollars.

The accompanying graph illustrates the difference deferring your taxes to a later date can make.

Tax-sheltering helps your money grow faster

While money doesn't grow on trees, it does grow much faster when it's invested in a tax-sheltered vehicle like an RRSP. The graph compares the growth of $5,000 per year, inside and outside an RRSP of someone in a 50% tax bracket. At the end of 25 years, the money invested in the RRSP is worth $394,772 — almost four times more than the non-sheltered investment.

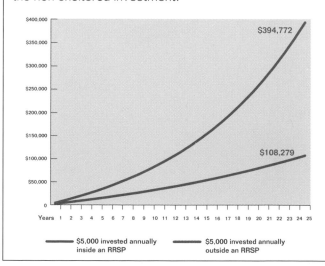

Tax-assisted savings plans

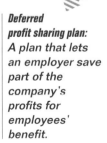

In addition to giving you an opportunity to generate wealth with money that otherwise would have gone to taxes, tax deferral can also lessen your total lifetime tax bill. The idea behind most tax deferral plans is to reduce the taxes paid during high-earning and high-tax paying years by not paying tax until retirement, when your income and tax rate may both be lower.

Pension adjustment:
The estimated current value of what your employer contributes to your defined benefit pension plan or deferred profit sharing plan.

Tax-assisted retirement savings plans come in several varieties including personal pension plans, RRSPs, and *deferred profit sharing plans* (DPSPs). RRSPs are subject to a contribution limit of 18% of earned income up to a maximum of $13,500 a year. However, if you have a company pension plan, or if your employer contributes to a DPSP on your behalf, this will reduce the amount you can put into your RRSP.

Figuring out your RRSP contribution room gets a bit trickier if you belong to a defined benefit pension plan — the kind that pays a certain percentage of salary for each year of service — or a DPSP. However, the government manages to put a dollar amount on the value by way of a calculation called the *pension adjustment* or PA. The employer's pension or DPSP contribution is used to calculate your pension adjustment. If your RRSP limit is $13,500 and your PA is $5,000, then you can contribute up to $8,500 to your RRSP.

Deferred profit sharing plan:
A plan that lets an employer save part of the company's profits for employees' benefit.

135

Always make the maximum RRSP contribution

No matter what type or combination of retirement savings plans you have, the key is to contribute your maximum each and every year. At the highest marginal tax rate, a $13,500 contribution to your RRSP, for instance, will save you about $6,750 in tax. That's equivalent to an immediate, risk-free gain on your investment of 50%! Better still, your investment continues to grow tax-free as long as it remains tax-sheltered. Chapter 20 provides more information about the various forms of tax-assisted retirement savings plans.

Planning for your children's education

Education costs are expected to rocket upwards in the future. Here's how to ensure your kids get the chances they deserve.

Give your kids the best

Almost from the time a new child comes home from the hospital, most parents start developing great expectations. We want our children to be loved. We want them to be successful. We want them to be fulfilled. In short, we want for them all the best that life offers. And while there is no single path to happiness, most parents realize that a solid education is one of the best investments they can make in their child's future.

Education opens up new vistas. In gives our children a chance to explore different ideas, discover new abilities and develop talents. It gives them a better chance at performing a worthwhile and respected role in the world. A good education has tremendous economic value and it's an asset they'll have for their entire lives.

In fact, your children's education will play a large part in determining their standard of living in our knowledge-based economy. We all know that a high

It pays to stay in school

Is higher education worth the investment? When it comes to future earning power, the answer is definitely yes.

Level of education	Average annual income
University graduates	$42,054
Some postsecondary education	$25,838
Less than Grade 9	$19,377

Source: Statistics Canada

school diploma no longer leads to a decent job and a
lifetime of relatively secure employment. We live in a
world in which new technology and growing global
markets drive the demand for an increasingly well-
educated workforce. A good education, now more than
ever, is the key to prosperity in a rapidly changing
world.

A good education isn't cheap

While children usually bring immeasurable joys, they
also present a major financial responsibility. In fact, if
you add it all up, the average cost of raising a child
born in Canada today could easily reach $160,000, and
that's only until age 18. Postsecondary education can
add significantly to the overall costs.

Since 1993, the average cost of university tuition
increased by more than 60% and it's expected to
significantly outpace inflation in the years ahead as
government subsidies decline further. And tuition fees
are just part of the bill. Experts estimate that a four-
year university education for a student who attends a
Canadian university in 2015 could well be around
$150,000 if the student lives away from home.

Another key question is how much of your child's
education are you able or willing to cover. There's a
good number of parents — and students — who
believe that when parents help out, the students
themselves should be responsible for at least a portion
of their postsecondary studies. Universities and
colleges usually are up front about the costs. And many
young people sock away much of their part-time

earnings for their education. Even if you can cover all their educational expenses, your kids might feel a greater sense of accomplishment and responsibility if they shoulder at least some of the cost.

How to estimate the cost of your children's education

This exercise isn't aimed for the faint of heart. The following worksheet on estimating the cost of your children's education covers most expenses, but remember, some of them may be much higher when your kids head off to college. While inflation assumptions can cover increases in living expenses and supplies, tuition could increase several times over in the next few years. The average tuition for an undergraduate arts program is more than $3,000 in Canada. In the U.S., tuition costs are considerably higher. The reason for the difference is that our government still subsidizes education. Based on recent history and the growing number of older people, that subsidy could be significantly reduced or eliminated.

With that warning in mind, here are some expenses to consider in estimating the cost of your children's education.

Education Expense Worksheet

Expense	Estimated Cost
Tuition	_____
Residence or other accommodation	_____
Lab or other educational costs	_____
Transportation/parking	_____
Car expenses	_____
Clothing and personal care	_____
Entertainment	_____
Transportation for periodic visits home	_____
Total	$_____

Educational assistance programs

Although a college or university education pays off in the long run, the costs can seem daunting. As in all other aspects of financial planning, there are some very effective strategies that can help you meet your goals, provided you have some time on your side. We'll take a look at the pros and cons of each of them, but before you start planning how to spend your own money, there are a number of educational assistance programs you should know about. The availability of these plans is

not always obvious so don't be afraid to do some
investigation.

University scholarships

Most universities offer scholarships for the academi-
cally inclined. Check with your high school guidance
counselor or universities for details. And, by the way,
don't forget to tell your children they'll need top marks.

On-campus employment

Many universities offer part-time, on-campus jobs in
maintenance, security, the bookstore, library, pubs and
other areas. Some of these jobs may be reserved for
students in need, so your child may have to prove
economic hardship to qualify. Of course, the part-time
job shouldn't be so onerous that it cuts into class or
study time.

Athletic scholarships

Many U.S. colleges and universities provide full
scholarships to gifted high school athletes. If you've got
a talented hockey or basketball player in the family,
you'd be wise to make some inquires. Canadian universities do not offer athletic scholarships.

Community and church groups
and private foundations

Many community organizations maintain scholarship
funds for the education of students in need. The high
school guidance office is probably the best place to
start looking for more information. Also check your
local newspaper or the information office at city hall.

Employer-sponsored assistance

Many large companies provide grants for the education
of employees' children. Although the amount of the
grant is modest, typically about $500 for each year of
school, it's nothing to sneeze at. And your kids may not
need to be at the top of the class to qualify. As well, if
you or your spouse works at a college or university, one
of the perks might be free tuition for your kids and
other immediate family members.

Student loans

All provinces sponsor student loan programs which
offer loans and perhaps grants. Student loans are
administered through the banks and are interest-free
until graduation. At that time the student is expected to
pay the loan back plus interest at the bank's prevailing
personal loan rate. Qualification is based on a means
test that examines the student's and the parents' financial resources. Your child can pick up a loan application at the high school guidance office.

Research via the Internet

Most, if not all, Canadian colleges and universities
have Web sites which offer speedy access to up-to-date
information about programs, student housing, on-
campus employment, special opportunities and other
topics of interest. The Association of Universities and
Colleges of Canada (AUCC) also has a site at
www.aucc.ca, while the Web address for the
Association of Community Colleges of Canada is
www.accc.ca. Each has information on post-secondary
education, plus links to its member organizations. The

AUCC Web site also has information on scholrships.

Each November, *Maclean's* magazine publishes a special feature on universities, offering information and rankings on programs, reputation, calibre of faculty and many other topics. You should be able to get a copy of this issue from your local library. As well, the *Maclean's* Web site at **www.macleans.ca** carries highlights of the special issue.

Chapter 19

Tax-smart education savings

Taking action now can help ensure your kids get the education they need.

Start early

Basically, there are three financial strategies that can help you prepare for the cost of your children's education:

1. paying off the mortgage;

2. setting up a registered education savings plan; and,

3. establishing an investment trust.

In this chapter, we'll take a look at the pros and cons of each approach.

Pay off the mortgage

Although paying off the mortgage doesn't sound like it has much to do with higher education, it's the informal funding approach favored by most Canadians. The idea is simple: your mortgage payment is likely your biggest single monthly expenditure, after paying the government taxes. If you can pay off your house before your first child goes to college or university, the extra cash flow may cover or offset the cost of tuition and living expenses.

From a strictly financial point of view this approach makes a lot of sense. After all, it would be hard to generate a guaranteed after-tax return on any investment equivalent to the interest you'll save by paying down your mortgage. However, there are some potential problems. Paying for school out of your future cash flow assumes you'll be gainfully employed when you need the money. Chances are you will be, but the economy is less certain than it once was. And what if your family is faced with bigger problems than unemployment? At the very least, you'll want to make sure that your life and disability insurance take the cost of your children's education into account.

If you do take this approach, also make sure that your mortgage is repaid before your kids head off to university. And if you can afford it, shorten the amorti-zation period so that your mortgage is paid sooner. That way, you can start directing all the money you're saving into a special savings or investment fund.

Start a registered education savings plan (RESP)

An RESP is an investment vehicle that gives you certain incentives to save for your children's education. Recent changes to the rules make RESPs more attractive than ever.

Canada Education Savings Grant: A government contribution to your RESP of up to $400 per year.

Under an RESP, you can contribute up to $4,000 a year (formerly $2,000) into a tax-sheltered fund for the education of each child. The total lifetime amount you can sock away for each child in $42,000. The big advantage of an RESP is that the gain on your invest-ment is tax-deferred. And as you can see in the chart on page 148, tax-deferred growth can make a huge difference in the return on your investment.

The federal government also provides a cash grant of 20% on your first $2,000 in contributions each year. That translates into an annual benefit of $400 per child. As the chart illustrates, the Canada Education Savings Grant gives your savings a substantial boost.

Under an RESP, all contributions — yours and the

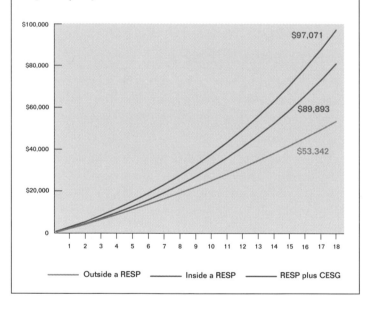

How education savings can grow

This graph compares what happens when $2,000 is invested each year for 18 years outside a RESP, inside a RESP, and when the same RESP investment is accompanied by the $400 Canada Education Savings Grant (CESG). These calculations are based on a annual interest rate of 8%. Since we've assumed a 50% marginal tax rate for the non-RESP investment, it actually grows at only 4% per year.

——— Outside a RESP   ——— Inside a RESP   ——— RESP plus CESG

government's — accumulate tax-free until your child begins their education at an accredited post-secondary institution. At that point, the assets of the fund are paid out in equal annual instalments and are taxed in the child's hands. Since students' incomes are generally low, the child may have little, if any, tax to pay.

RESPs are a tax-effective way to save for your

child's education. The increase in the contribution limit and the introduction of the Canada Education Savings Grant make them more attractive than ever. However, RESPs can still contain many different restrictions you need to know.

Beware of the fine print in RESPs
The original and most common type of RESP is the scholarship trust. Typically, they allow monthly contributions between $20 to $300 and invest your money in secure, fixed-income securities such as government bonds, mortgage-backed securities and guaranteed investment certificates. Originally, scholarship trusts contained a few potentially onerous restrictions such as forfeiting all the earnings on your contributions if your child didn't end up going to college. The proceeds would remain in the pool and be used to sweeten the payout for students who carried on with their education. While most parents are sure that their budding geniuses will earn an undergraduate degree at the very least, your child may not go to university. If that's the case, and you belong to such a plan, only your contributions will be returned to you. After many years of tax-deferred compounding, what you get back might represent less than half of the accumulated wealth in the RESP.

Since the federal government changed the rules, the entire value of the RESP can be transferred to another sibling without a tax penalty, or failing that, be eligible for transfer to your RRSP in an amount up to $40,000 (provided the plan is at least 10 years old and the student is at least 21 years old).

Of course, you have to make sure that your RESP takes advantage of the new rules. Even if it does, you might not be able to take advantage of all the new flexibility they offer. For example, the transferability of funds to your RRSP only benefits you if you have unused RRSP contribution room. If you don't have room in your RRSP, you can still cash the RESP if your plan allows, but you'll have to pay tax on the difference between its present value and the amount of your contributions at your marginal tax rate plus a 20% additional tax. This translates into a tax hit of more than 70% if you are in the top marginal tax rate.

RRSP contribution room: Accumulated amount that you can contribute to your RRSP; can be carried without limit to future years.

Remember, too, that most RESPs still contain fairly narrow definitions of "accredited school of learning." If your child decides to become a massage therapist, she may not be eligible for benefits. Always make sure you read the fine print.

Consider self-directed RESPs

Because the rate of return on scholarship funds has traditionally been limited by the low-risk nature of the securities in which they were invested, many brokers, mutual fund dealers and financial institutions developed self-directed RESPs for their clients. Like the name implies, you can direct your contributions into a wide range of potential investments including stocks, bonds and mutual funds. If you have a long investment horizon, the potential return, and thus the amount of money you'll have available when it comes time for college, can be much greater.

Open a trust account

While RESPs are more flexible than ever before, they still come with quite a few strings attached. If you don't like these limitations, opening a investment account in the name of your child — sometimes referred to as an informal trust — might be the answer. The beauty of this is that any contributions you make belong to your child whether or not they go to college or university.

Trust:
An account in the name of a person called a trustee held for the benefit of another person.

Attribution rules:
When investment income is earned by one person but taxed in the hands of the previous owner.

You have to be careful, however, to consider the attribution rules mentioned in Chapter 16. Briefly stated, they specify that any income earned on your contributions would be attributed back to you for tax purposes. However, the attribution rules make an exception when it comes to capital gains. If you make sure your trust is invested in a growth-oriented Canadian equity fund, for example, you can expect most of the fund's increase in value to come from capital gains. You still will be responsible for paying tax on the interest income generated by the fund, but your child pays the tax on capital gains, and invariably at a much lower tax rate.

Establish a formal trust

Of course, the downside of an informal trust account is that legally, your son or daughter can use the money you have carefully set aside for their higher education to buy a Harley or travel to Katmandu. To prevent that from happening, you'll have to establish a formal trust that sets out the specific terms and conditions for the use of the trust fund. You will need the help of a lawyer to make sure everything is in order and you will have to file a special tax return every year, but the benefits and tax implications of a formal trust are otherwise the same as an informal trust account.

Top up your RRSP first

Which strategy is best for you? If you already make your maximum RRSP contribution, and your mortgage is well in hand, and you are looking for more ways to shelter your income, RESPs or trust accounts might make sense. Both vehicles contain considerable tax advantages. And you may find peace of mind knowing that funds have been earmarked for educating your children.

Remember, though, that if you are not already making maximum use of your RRSP, you should probably think carefully before setting up a RESP or trust account. The tax-deductibility of RRSP contributions, at the highest marginal tax rate, is equivalent to an immediate 50% gain on your investment. It may make more sense to get that money working toward your retirement early and worry about the children's education later. By the same token, your kids may be better served in the long run if you are able to retire your mortgage early.

Registered retirement savings plans

Learn the ins and outs of RRSPs so you can have the retirement you've dreamed of.

The onus is on you

When registered retirement savings plans were introduced in 1957, the federal government wanted Canadians to begin recognizing the need to save for their own retirements. Today, that need is greater than ever.

Employer-sponsored pension plans cover a smaller percentage of the workforce than when RRSPs were first introduced, and the government-sponsored retirement benefits — once considered sacrosanct — have already been scaled back. Meanwhile, the debate on how to fund future obligations to CPP and QPP is well under way. Premiums have already started to go up and a variety of other scenarios including a higher retirement age and lower benefits are under serious consideration. Amid this uncertainty, one thing is clear. Taking maximum advantage of your RRSP is more important than ever.

Employer-sponsored pension plan:
A retirement plan provided by your employer to which both you and the company contribute.

Why RRSPs are such good things

You can direct up to 18% of your previous year's income to a maximum of $13,500, less the value of any contributions made by you or your employer toward a group RRSP or pension plan.

The reason RRSPs are so popular, of course, is that they contain two powerful tax benefits. First, the annual contribution is immediately tax deductible which means that if you are at the highest marginal tax rate, your taxes are reduced by more than 50 cents for each dollar you contribute. Better still, the earnings on your contributions are tax-sheltered as long as they remain in the plan. We'll see just how great a

difference these two benefits can make to boosting your
retirement in a moment.

How much can you contribute?

You can contribute up to 18% of our previous year's
earned income, to a maximum of $13,500.
Understanding how earned income is defined is important, since it determines exactly how much you can sock
away each year. Earned income for the purpose of
RRSP contributions is the total of:

- all employment income (less union or professional
  dues);

- net rental income;

- net income from self-employment;

- royalties;

- research grants;

- alimony or maintenance payments;

- disability payments from CPP or QPP; and,

- supplementary EI payments.

You can carry-forward unused room
While the current RRSP limits are rather generous,
many people have trouble coming up with the money to
take advantage of them every year. In days past, taxpayers who failed to make the maximum contribution
in a given year lost their opportunity forever. Today,
however, the federal government allows you to carry
any unused contribution room forward without
restriction. This can be a boon to taxpayers who come
into large chunks of cash from an inheritance, for

example, but be careful. It may not be to your advantage to sock your windfall into an RRSP all at once. Since the tax benefits of the RRSP contribution are most pronounced in the highest tax bracket, it might make sense to spread a large chunk of unused contribution room over more than one year. On the other hand, you have to balance the benefit of maximizing your tax deductions against the benefit of giving your contributions extra time to compound in value.

RRSP overcontribution: An excess contribution to an RRSP for which you pay a one per cent penalty a month on any amount over $2,000.

The best strategy is to make the contribution sooner rather than later whenever you can. You may not be able to take advantage of unused contribution room in the future. It's seldom easier to come up with a larger sum for investment later. Besides, there is nothing to prevent the government from restricting or eliminating the carry-forward provision in a future budget.

You can also overcontribute

Now that the government spells out your annual RRSP contribution limit, as well as any unused contribution room soon after you've completed your tax return, it's very unlikely to unknowingly overcontribute to your RRSP. However, some people will do it on purpose as a tax planning tool. Essentially, you can overcontribute to your RRSP by up to $2,000 without attracting any adverse consequences. Beyond that, however, you have to be reasonably certain that the benefit of the extra contribution more than offsets the penalty tax, which is 1% per month on any overcontribution in excess of $2,000. If you overcontribute as much as $2,000, it can't be deducted from your income to reduce tax until some future time when you do have the contribution room. Still, you benefit from the tax-sheltered growth of your overcontribution.

Off-the-shelf RRSPs

There are many different types of RRSPs. Knowing what each type is all about will help you find the one that's right for you. Most of the savings and investment vehicles offered by Canadian financial institutions are available in an RRSP-eligible version. To qualify, they must be registered with Revenue Canada as an RRSP and they must satisfy minimum Canadian investment content rules. A wide range of investments can be held in an RRSP including savings accounts, GICs and mutual funds. The advantage of these so-called off-the-shelf RRSPs is that you won't have to spend a lot of time managing your investments.

Self-directed RRSPs

An option for people who choose to take a more active role in managing their investments is the self-directed RRSP. A self-directed RRSP is a personal, all-inclusive retirement savings account. It lists all your holdings on one monthly statement — no matter how your money is invested — and it shows exactly how your assets are diversified between different investment categories such as cash and equities or domestic and international. As such, self-directed RRSPs provide a handy snapshot of your total portfolio. This makes it easier to keep track of your returns and to ensure your assets are weighted to take account of changing economic conditions.

The cost of all this convenience and flexibility is relatively modest. Most brokers charge about $100 a year to administer a self-directed RRSP, although many will waive the fee depending on the size of your account. In most cases, fees are waived when you have $20,000 or more in the account.

Any of the individual RRSP products offered by various financial institutions can be held in a self-directed RRSP. But it can also hold many other investments, including the common shares of individual public companies. Here is a list of the most common assets you can put in a self-directed RRSP:

- guaranteed investment certificates;
- mutual funds;
- bonds and debentures;
- common shares; and
- a mortgage on Canadian real estate (including your own mortgage).

Transferring assets into a self-directed RRSP
A self-directed RRSP has one other amazing benefit: it allows you to transfer assets you already own into it. This means you can qualify for a tax deduction without spending money. For instance, let's say you are in the highest tax bracket and own $5,000 in common shares of a Canadian company. If you were to transfer the shares into your RRSP, you would qualify for a tax refund of about $2,500. All without spending a cent!

The value of any securities or assets transferred

into your self-directed RRSP, for tax purposes, is deemed to be their fair market value on the date of transfer. If securities are transferred into a self-directed RRSP, there are some other tax consequences you should know:

Deemed disposition: *When you are treated as having sold an asset even though no sale has actually taken place.*

- the transfer of assets is classified as a deemed disposition;

- if the market value of the transferred assets is higher than their original cost, you have to pay capital gains tax on the difference;

- if the market value is lower than the original cost, you cannot claim a capital loss; and,

- if a debt security, such as a bond, is contributed between interest payment dates, the amount of the contribution will include all amounts accrued until the date of transfer. This same accrued interest must also be included in your taxable income for the year in which you make the contribution.

Is a self-directed RRSP right for you?

If you like the idea of taking an active role in the management of your investments, a self-directed RRSP might be right for you. Remember, though, that no matter how much you enjoy looking after your own affairs, the ultimate objective of owning a self-directed RRSP should be to outperform the market. If you aren't confident of doing that, it might make more sense to buy a portfolio of the various RRSP products available. The other consideration, of course, is that your self-directed RRSP should be large enough to warrant the annual administration fee you may be charged.

Actively manage only part of your money
Since no one becomes an investment expert overnight, many people hedge their bets by holding mostly mutual funds within their self-directed RRSPs, and taking a more active role in managing the balance of the portfolio. Most self-directed RRSPs have access to a wide and growing range of mutual funds and with each you get the benefit of professional management and, theoretically, investment performance which generally reflects the overall market. At the same time, the self-directed RRSP gives you the flexibility to personally manage a portion of your investment nest egg and a chance to augment your returns by investing in a small number of hand-picked securities.

Advantages of RRSPs

Without a doubt, the RRSP is the single nicest thing the Canadian government has ever done for taxpayers. The greatest immediate benefit of RRSPs is that you can deduct RRSP contributions from your taxable income, then use any resulting refund to contribute to your RRSP in the current year. This is like getting the government to finance your retirement plan.

Get immediate and ongoing tax deductions
Because it's a deduction — and not a tax credit — the higher your marginal tax rate, the more your RRSP contribution will save in income tax. For instance, if you're in a 50% (combined federal and provincial rate) tax bracket, a $10,000 RRSP contribution will save you about $5,000 in tax. That's equivalent to an immediate 50% gain on your investment. If you take

this tax-saving benefit to the maximum and invest your rebate, you are even further ahead.

Benefit from long-term tax deferral

The other primary benefit of RRSPs is long-term tax deferral. As we said, any income or capital gains generated by your RRSP is sheltered from tax as long as they remain in the plan. If you recall the chart from chapter 17, tax-free compounding within the RRSP is one of the fastest ways to a comfortable retirement.

Score tax savings in the future

Because an RRSP enables you to defer tax until retirement, presumably both your income and the tax you eventually pay on it will be lower.

Split income through a spousal RRSP

Spousal RRSPs give working couples the chance to transfer income from the highest to lowest income earner, thus lowering the amount of total tax paid by the family.

The chance to receive lump-sum income tax-free

If you stop working for any reason and at any age, you can transfer your retiring allowance tax-free into your RRSP. Retiring allowances are up to $2,000 per year up to and including 1995, plus $1,500 per year up to and including 1988 when employer contributions did not vest with you.

'Disadvantages' of RRSPs

While RRSPs offer powerful tax-assisted benefits, they do contain a few potential limitations which you should know. For instance:

- when funds are withdrawn from your RRSP, you pay income tax on all the proceeds at your full tax rate. This is the case even though some of the money may have been earnings through capital gains or dividends from Canadian corporations, both of which otherwise qualify for special tax breaks. It's therefore important that you have alternate funds set up for emergencies;

Retiring allowance:
An amount you may get from your employer when you retire, or upon the death of your spouse.

Withholding tax:
Tax that is deducted by your financial institution or employer when you withdraw funds from a registered plan.

- funds withdrawn from an RRSP are subject to a minimum federal withholding tax of 10% to 30% (18% to 35% for Quebec residents);

- if you die early, all assets in your RRSP are deemed to be liquidated at the time of death and are subject to tax unless they are to be received by your spouse or, under certain circumstances, a dependent child or grandchild;

- if a whole life insurance policy is registered as an RRSP, the policyholder cannot take out policy loans from the insurer and the policy can't be used as collateral;

- none of the assets of an RRSP can be used as collateral for a loan; and,

- except for segregated funds, RRSPs do not offer potential protection from creditors.

How to mature your RRSP

Maturing an RRSP means winding up the plan and

arranging to receive all the funds that have
accumulated. While an RRSP can be wound up any
time you like, it must be matured by the end of
the year in which you reach your 69th birthday.

When it comes time to wind up your RRSP,
you have several options, and each affects the
amount of money you receive, the time you
receive it, and the tax you pay on it. It's
therefore a good idea to give some advance
consideration to the three basic maturity options
that are available.

RRIF: Registered Retirement Income Fund: *An investment account to which you transfer RRSPs to provide a series of minimum payments based on a prescribed government formula.*

1. Withdraw all proceeds as a lump sum

Sometimes referred to as collapsing or cashing
in your RRSP, this option is subject to the withholding
tax and you must pay income tax on the full amount in
your RRSP in the year you collapse it. This option
might be suitable if you really need to get your hands
on the cash but it probably will keep you from taking
advantage of the tax savings from spreading your
income over several years.

2. Transfer RRSP proceeds into a registered retirement income fund (RRIF)

This option enables you to further extend the tax
deferral benefits of your RRSP since tax is paid only on
the income you withdraw each year. Similar to RRSPs,
RRIFs can be purchased from most banks, trust
companies and life insurance companies. Most of the
investment products offered by these institutions are
RRIF-eligible and thus you can pick and choose from a
full range of cash, fixed-income and equity products.

RRIFs are also available as self-directed plans.

The main advantage of a RRIF is that, similar to an RRSP, it provides a way to shelter income on funds until they are withdrawn from the plan. Compared to other retirement income options, the RRIF offers control over your capital with some flexibility in how much you have to withdraw from the fund. Here's how RRIFs work.

The rules for RRIFs

You must withdraw a minimum annual amount and it's taxable when received. There is no maximum withdrawal.

For RRIFs established before 1993, and for RRIF holders aged 78 or younger, the minimum amount that must be withdrawn each year equals the value of the RRIF's assets at the beginning of the calendar year divided by the number of years until the planholder turns 90. Assume that on January 1 of year three, a 74-year old has $100,000 of assets in a RRIF. The minimum amount that has to be withdrawn that year is $100,000 divided by 16 (90 minus 74), or $6,250. Under these rules, the RRIF would be fully depleted once the planholder turns 90.

Since some people live a long time, the government set new rules for RRIFs started after 1992, or for RRIF holders age 79 or older. The minimum amount that must be withdrawn is a fraction that increases gradually each year, eventually leveling off at 20% of the value of the RRIF's assets once you, or your spouse if he or she is younger, reach age 94.

Except for prescribed minimum payments, RRIFs

RRIFs let you manage your money in retirement to ensure continued tax-sheltered growth.

offer a lot of flexibility. You can vary the income flow by choosing a minimum, level or indexed payment. You can also customize the income flow to meet your own needs by specifying annual, semi-annual, quarterly or monthly payments. And because you can withdraw any amount above the minimum whenever you want, RRIFs allow you to fund major expenses such as a car or vacation when the need arises.

What happens if your RRIF outlives you?
Accumulated amounts in a RRIF must be included in the income of the planholder in the year of death unless:

- the funds are transferred to a dependent child or grandchild; or

- the RRIF is transferred directly to a surviving spouse, in which case the RRIF payments are taxable in the spouse's hands. As an alternative, the

165

surviving spouse can use the accumulated amounts
to buy another RRIF or an annuity.

3. Transfer the proceeds to buy an annuity

RRSP proceeds may also be used to purchase an
annuity. An annuity is a contract for a guaranteed
series of payments. It can be used to convert the value
of your RRSP into a regular income for any period of
time you choose, including your entire life. The amount
you receive depends on the size of your deposit, your
age, interest rates in effect at the time you purchase the
annuity, and the type of annuity you select.

Annuity:
*A retirement
vehicle that
gives you a
guaranteed
income stream
for life or to a set
date in return for
a lump sum
payment.*

Annuities are a popular choice for some people at
retirement because, unlike RRIFs, they can guarantee
that you won't outlive your income and they require no
further investment decisions.

Of course, you can win or lose on your
"investment." Essentially, the insurance or
trust company that issues it estimates how
much it can afford to pay you every month
based on the amount of your deposit, their
potential return, and how long you'll likely live.
If you live longer than expected, you'll make
out nicely because you'll collect more than
warranted, based on the amount of your deposit.
Conversely, if you fail to reach average life expectancy,
the insurance company keeps the balance and uses it
to pay its older customers.

To mitigate the horror of being run over by a bus on
the way out of the insurance company's office, many
people buy annuities that are modified to pay for life, or
for a specified minimum period such as 10 years. As you

Types of Annuities

Although there are many variations, there are three common annuity types:

Term Certain Annuity: Guarantees payments for 5, 10, 15, or 20 years, although you can specify any term. Payments are a blend of interest and principal, with all the capital returned over the term. If you die during the term, payments continue to the stated beneficiary to the contract's end.

Single Life Annuity: Gives you the assurance that you will never outlive your income. Provides the highest guaranteed income of all annuities, but all payments end on your death.

Joint Life and Survivor Annuity: Continues to pay, as long as you or your spouse are living. Based on two lives, payments continue to the survivor's death.

might expect, the monthly income associated with such plans is correspondingly lower.

Interestingly enough, while evidence of good health gets you a better rate for life insurance, evidence of bad health can get you a better rate on an annuity. If you can prove that you have a diminished life expectancy, you may be able to earn a higher monthly benefit.

The tax implications for registered annuities are similar to RRIFs. Income is included in your taxable income as received and tax is automatically withheld by the financial institution that issues it.

Comparing features of different Annuities

Features	Fixed-term	Single-life	Joint & last survivor
Income	Equal amounts paid to age 90.	Paid for life of single annuitant.	Pays until both the annuitant and annuitant's spouse die.
Access to capital	Yes, but penalties apply.	None	None
Coverage for spouse	Yes	None	Yes
Estate protection period.	Yes, residual amounts commuted and paid to estate if annuitant dies before age 90.	If bought with guarantee period. When you die within guarantee period, residual amount is paid to estate	If bought with guarantee
Equal income by gender	Yes	None	None

Government and employer-sponsored pension plans

What can you rely on the government and your
employer to provide during your golden years?

Government pension plans

As we mentioned, the aging of the country's population and the heightened sense of job insecurity in the workplace have motivated many Canadians to take more personal responsibility for funding their retirement. However, the fact remains that for most retiring Canadians, the traditional government and employer-sponsored pension plans continue to form the bulk of their retirement income.

Most of us have only a vague awareness of the pension benefits to which we will be entitled. Yet, it's important to know what you can look forward to in retirement so you can prepare for any shortfall as early as possible and determine if the RRSP income we talked about in the previous chapter will prove sufficient. Let's have a look at each of the major sources of government-provided retirement income.

Old Age Security (OAS)

The Old Age Security pension is payable at age 65 to all Canadian citizens and legal residents. The amount is reviewed quarterly to take into account increases in inflation. In 1999, the maximum OAS benefit was $410.82 per month.

OAS is payable to all Canadians regardless of income level, but higher income earners must repay all or part of the OAS benefit. Essentially, an individual with a net income above $53,215 must repay at least a portion of the OAS benefit, and the higher the net income, the higher the percentage of OAS to be repaid. Once you hit around $80,000 in net income, all social

Where today's seniors get their money

Government pensions make up the larges source of
income for sneiors today. With the future of these
programs in question, it's crucial that Canadians raise their
level of personal investment or continue working later into
their lives.

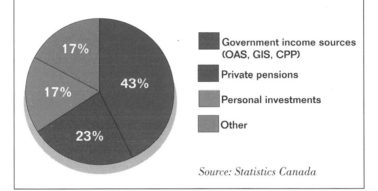

Government income sources
(OAS, GIS, CPP)

Private pensions

Personal investments

Other

Source: Statistics Canada

benefits including OAS must be paid back when you
file your income tax return.

Guaranteed Income Supplement (GIS)

Originally designed as a temporary measure to help
low-income seniors until the Canada Pension Plan was
established, the GIS has continued to this day.
However, it isn't easy to get.

To qualify, you must be an OAS recipient with no
other income or limited income. The amount of the
benefit is determined by marital status and base
income. In 1999, the maximum monthly GIS benefit
was $488.23 for a single pensioner and $318.01 each

171

for married pensioners. Benefits are not taxable. Like OAS, GIS benefits have been adjusted quarterly since 1973 to reflect changes in the Consumer Price Index.

The Canada and Quebec pension plans

The Canada Pension Plan (CPP) was established in 1965 as a national social insurance program to provide retirement, disability and survivor benefits. Quebec has its own pension plan (QPP), and the CPP and QPP are closely coordinated and are portable from one province to another.

CPP is known as a "contributory" plan. Payments to today's pensions are funded through contributions made to the plan by employees, their employers and self-employed people, plus the interest earned on the investment of these contributions. That's OK until the ratio of pensioners to contributors rises. And that's exactly what's been happening for many years. As well, a huge increase in claims for disability pensions has put the CPP under added stress.

Eventually something has to give — usually the taxpayer. The debate on various solutions for the under-funding of CPP has already begun. These include increased contributions, reduced benefits, a higher retirement age and various combinations thereof. In the meantime, here's how the system works.

Your benefit at retirement will be determined by the total amount of contributions made over your working lifetime. Contributions are payable only on amounts of income to the Yearly Maximum Pensionable

Earnings (YMPE). The amount changes each year and is $37,400 in 1999. Any amount of income you earn in excess of that amount is neither subject to premiums nor eligible for benefits.

How to calculate your CPP benefit

The amount of retirement pension is equal to 25% of your average monthly pensionable earnings during the period you contributed to CPP. Once you start receiving it, the CPP benefit is adjusted annually based on changes in the Consumer Price Index.

In 1999, the maximum monthly CPP retirement benefit payable to a person aged 65 is $751.67. This figure is determined by calculating the average YMPE over the past five years (1995, 1996, 1997, 1998 and 1999) and dividing by 12:

$$\frac{(\$34,900 + \$35,400 + \$35,800 + \$36,900 + \$37,400) \div 5}{12}$$

$$= \$3,006.66$$

Therefore, the maximum CPP retirement pension is 25% of that amount, or $751.67.

Of course, whether you qualify for the maximum benefit also depends on how long and how much you've contributed.

Early or late retirement

Contributors to CPP may apply for pension benefits as early as age 60 if they stop working, but a discount applies to the monthly benefit. Between the ages of 60 and 65, the amount of pension is reduced by 0.5% for each month preceding the pensioner's 65th birthday, and the reduction remains in effect throughout the pensioner's lifetime.

Conversely, if you don't need the money right away, you can postpone CPP pension benefits to as late as age 70. In this case, your pension is higher. After age 65, the amount of monthly pension payable is increased by 0.5% for each month the pension is delayed. The maximum increase is 30%.

Understanding your company's pension plan

Vesting:
Your right to all or part of your employer's contributions to your pension plan.

All employer-sponsored pensions fit into one of two general categories: defined benefit or defined contribution plans. In a defined benefit plan, the pension benefit you receive at retirement is known in advance. The company is obliged to add money to the pension fund as required, to ensure there's sufficient money to pay the promised pension benefits. Conversely, in a defined contribution plan, it's the final pension benefit you receive at retirement that's uncertain. The only thing that's known is the amount of money you put into the plan. Your employer has no obligation to ensure a certain pension benefit.

Most Canadians covered by employer-sponsored pensions belong to defined benefit plans. Typically, these plans promise to pay a certain percentage of your final salary for each year of service. Traditionally, defined benefit plans treated long-term employees quite generously, whereas short-term employees, or

What types of pension plans do Canadians have?

Most employees in Canada are covered by defined benefit plans (88.1%). However, defined contribution plans are becoming increasingly popular.

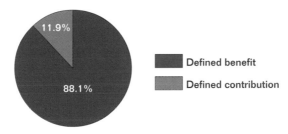

Source: Statistics Canada, Pension Plans in Canada 1996.

those who work for several companies in a lifetime, were treated less favorably.

To make things fairer, the government introduced significant pension reform in 1988. Among other things, it was designed to provide an increasingly mobile workforce with earlier vesting of pension benefits (entitlement to employer contributions) and enhanced portability.

In response to the increased administrative burden and extra costs involved, many employers have subsequently phased out defined benefit plans and replaced them with defined contribution plans. Although many younger employees embrace defined contribution plans because they can see the exact value of employer contributions, many older employees — for reasons we'll explore in a moment — recognize that defined benefit plans are usually more valuable in the long run.

Defined benefit pension plans

Defined benefit pension plans come in three basic types: flat benefit plans, career average plans, and final average plans.

Flat benefit plans

This is by far the simplest type of defined benefit pension plan, with the monthly pension being a specified amount of dollars for each year of service. A plan specifying $15 per year of service would produce a pension of $450 per month after 30 years. This type of pension is common among unionized employees where wage levels are generally uniform.

Although this type of plan is easy to understand, it's the least desirable type of defined benefit pension plan. Because it pays a flat benefit, it doesn't automatically reflect increases in earnings. What's worse, because the benefit amount is established in today's dollars, it offers no automatic protection against inflation. The flat amount may be increased by subsequent contract negotiations, but there's no guarantee.

Career average plans

This type of plan calculates the pension benefit as a percentage of the employee's career earnings. For example, the plan might specify that an employee is entitled to 2% of earnings for each year of service as a member of the plan. If the employee has 30 years of service and average monthly earnings of $1,000 over that time, the pension payable at retirement would be $600 a month (2% x $1,000 x 30 years).

While taking the employee's entire career into account might seem beneficial, this plan is very vulnerable to the effects of inflation. Many companies with career average plans update the base year in the pension formula from time to time, if they can afford to do so. For example, if the base year is moved forward to 1994, all service prior to 1994 will be based on 1994 earnings rather than actual earnings.

Final average plans
Similar to career average plans, the final average plan bases the pension on a combination of length of service and earnings. However, rather than basing the earnings over a lifetime of service, final average plans use a specified period of time. Often, this is the average of the best five consecutive years of earnings in the last 10 years of employment or perhaps the best three consecutive years of earnings in the last five years of employment. Final average plans are considered the best type of defined benefit pension plan because they provide a high degree of protection against inflation right up to retirement.

Defined contribution (money purchase) pension plans
In this type of plan, the employer contributes a fixed percentage based on the employee's annual earnings. Most often, the expense of funding such a plan is shared, with employees contributing a percentage of their salary and the employer matching it, subject to certain limits. The pension at retirement is whatever

amount the accumulated contributions and interest will
buy in annuities. Annuity purchases can be made each
year or at the time of retirement.

As you might expect, defined contribution plans
are popular with employers because they're easy to
administer and generally are less costly. Many
employees also like them because they have the
flexibility to direct their contributions within a range of
investments.

All this convenience, however, comes with a
higher degree of risk and uncertainty for many
employees. Although contributions are defined, the
ultimate retirement benefit isn't known until retirement. At that point, the final pension may be much
smaller or, for that matter, much larger than expected.
Also, because employees have some flexibility in the
way their contributions are invested, members retiring
in essentially the same circumstances can have
substantially different pensions.

Vesting — when employer contributions become yours

A wide range of vesting rules in various pension plans
used to govern whether a dismissed or resigning
employee received some of the employer's pension
contributions. Traditionally, these rules favored long-
term employees, and this seemed natural since the
objective of any employee benefit program is to attract
and retain good staff. Typically, pension benefits
forfeited by employees who didn't stick around for at

least 10 years were used to sweeten the pot for long-
service employees.

Trouble was, employees who spent their careers
with a number of companies found they weren't entitled
to any significant pension benefits at retirement. Partly
in response to this problem, the federal government
introduced pension legislation in the 1980s that
contained minimum vesting provisions. Today, federal
pension laws and those of Nova Scotia, Quebec,
Ontario, British Columbia, Saskatchewan and Manitoba
require full vesting or entitlement to employer
contributions for any employment period or
plan membership of more than two years. The
law is less generous in other provinces.

You have to transfer to a locked-in account

Now that more employees are entitled to their
employers' accumulated pension contributions,
the question of what do with all that money
arises. Not surprisingly, the government believes that
the original purpose of those contributions — that is to
fund a secure retirement — should be respected.
Accordingly, under both federal and provincial pension
legislation, an individual can't take the money in cash.
Instead, the funds must be transferred into a special
locked-in RRSP which remains off limits until
retirement. Otherwise the individual still owns the
funds and can invest them with all the flexibility
accorded other RRSPs.

Locked-in account: *An account set up for money transferred from a registered pension plan; cannot be use for non-retirement purposes.*

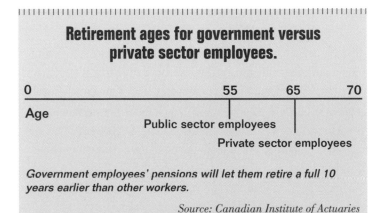

Retirement ages for government versus private sector employees.

0		55	65	70

Age   Public sector employees

Private sector employees

Government employees' pensions will let them retire a full 10 years earlier than other workers.

Source: Canadian Institute of Actuaries

Government employees have the fattest pensions of all Canadians. In fact, although they make up only a quarter of the workforce, public sector employees own almost 70% of pension assets in the country.

What does this mean? Well, a Canadian Institute of Actuaries study found that public servants are so well off that they will be able to retire on average 10 years earlier than private sector workers.

The Association of Canadian Pension Managers (ACPM) blames the skewed picture mostly on unfair government policies written by government employees which favor government pensions over private plans. Says an ACPM paper on the issue: "If we want our retirement system to meet the needs of all Canadians, we need policies at both the federal and provincial levels that apply fairly and equally to the public and private sectors."

Group RRSPs becoming more popular

Why, you may be asking, is this topic covered here rather than in the previous chapter on RRSPs? The

reason, of course, is the growing popularity of group
RRSPs as an alternative to traditional employer-
sponsored pension plans.

With the advent of pension reform, many
employers have replaced defined-benefit with defined-
contribution plans. Group RRSPs take the process one
step further because, while they can be set up much
like a defined contribution plan, they are not encum-
bered by pension laws.

The primary attraction of group RRSPs usually is
the employer contribution. It's frequently set up as a
matching contribution with a structure very similar to a
defined contribution pension plan. For example, it
might specify that any contribution made by the
employee up to 5% of earnings is matched by the
employer. The maximum amount that can be contributed to a group RRSP is usually subject to your
overall RRSP limit (18% of earned income up to a
maximum of $13,500). In this example, total employer
and employee contributions to the group plan would be
10% of income, which would leave contribution room
of 8% of income for personal RRSPs. Of course, if your
group RRSP is attractive in its own right, you may want
to make your entire annual RRSP contribution through
the group plan.

Another benefit of group RRSPs is payroll
deduction. Because contributions are made each pay
period, your money goes to work for you immediately.
At the same time, you get immediate tax relief on your
deductions, rather than waiting for a refund on your
lump-sum contribution at the end of the tax year.

Whether you decide to take full advantage of the group RRSP also depends on its performance relative to other RRSP options. Group RRSPs often contain a wide range of investment choices, including money market, fixed-income and equity mutual fund investments. So, if you have access to a group RRSP, chances are it will contain an investment option compatible with your objectives.

Chapter 22

How much will you need to retire?

Determine your retirement expenses and income to highlight any shortfall you need to plan for.

Three steps in retirement strategy

Now that we've had a look at all the potential sources of retirement income, it's time to establish a retirement strategy that meets your particular circumstances. There are three basic steps in the process.

1. Estimate your total retirement income
The first step is to determine how much after-tax income you will get when you retire. Include income from all government programs such as CPP and QPP, employer-sponsored pension and other retirement income programs, and from other sources such as investment or rental income or part-time employment.

2. Estimate your anticipated retirement needs
The second step is to decide how much after-tax income you'll need. This largely depends on your chosen lifestyle and your age at retirement. If you aren't sure what your needs will be, it's best to pick a target based on a percentage of your pre-retirement income. Although most financial planners suggest a target of 70%, it's probably wise to shoot a bit higher if you can. People are living longer and it's surprising how fast money can go when you have time to spend it.

Generally, retirees find certain expenses significantly reduced while other expenses are higher. The table opposite provides a few examples to think about.

Once you've had a chance to consider the effect that retirement will have on your living expenses, compare your estimated income and deductions just

What to expect when you retire

Probable lower expenses	Probable higher expenses
clothing	health and dental care and drugs*
commuting costs	life insurance*
accommodation	recreational travel
wardrobe/household cleaning	hobbies

*if benefits through employer-sponsored plans don't continue

before retirement with those just after retirement. For example, if your goal is to generate 80% of pre-retirement net income and your estimates reveal that you'll need more than that to fund the lifestyle you want, the difference between the two figures will have to come from personal savings.

3. Establish a retirement savings program as soon as possible

The final step is to establish a program to help you reach your savings goal. Most important is to decide what percentage of current income you can set aside to meet that pre-tax savings objective, and how long it will realistically take to achieve it. Next, you must decide how your savings will be invested. Finally, re-trace these steps every few years to ensure that your retirement plan is still on target.

Analyzing your
retirement income needs

This section and the worksheet on page 188 are
designed to help you estimate your own retirement
income and expenses, as well as any savings that might
be required to meet your objectives. While it's fairly
straightforward to pinpoint what your RRSPs,
investments and savings are worth today (see
worksheet), the calculations to project their value when
you do retire — which could be some time down the
road — are rather tricky. Similarly, while it shouldn't
be too hard to estimate your retirement expenses in
today's dollars the math to project those costs in
retirement is again rather advanced. Instead of wading
through complex formulas, we suggest you visit some
Web sites of banks and other financial instititutions.
Many if not all of these sites have special calculators or
programs that will crunch the numbers for you, once
you supply the required information. When you have
the numbers you need, simply add them in the
appropriate spaces on the worksheet. A list of useful
Web sites is included in the appendix on page 200.

Alternately, you could enlist the help of a financial
advisor to help you get the numbers you need, and the
next chapter talks about financial advisors and how to
find one. Given the importance of this excerise, you
may want to consult an advisor even if you use Web
sites or other means to get the figures you need.

Meeting the shortfall

If you are like most Canadians, this exercise will

probably identify a shortfall between how much it will cost to fund your retirement, and how much you'll have available. Remember, too, this is only a snapshot. The amount of income you can depend on from government sources may be much lower by the time you retire, so it pays to go through this exercise at least every few years.

If you have identified a shortfall, and you aren't planning on winning the lottery, you'll have to develop one of the following strategies to solve your problem:

Make maximum use of your RRSP or pension plan

If you aren't already making the maximum allowable contribution to your RRSP or pension plan, this is the most effective place to direct your savings.

Resolve to start saving more

Increasing the amount of money you save will probably entail a thorough review, and possibly a reduction of monthly expenditures, but it's not the end of the world. A more austere budget will force you to choose between non-essential current expenditures and a better standard of living at retirement.

Consider increasing your equity exposure

If you have the time to ride out fluctuations in the market, a hard analysis of your current situation might cause you to consider moving more of your investment portfolio into more aggressive assets such as equities. As we have seen, they entail a higher degree of risk than fixed-income and other types of investments, but the rewards, if you have enough time to wait for them, can significantly boost your retirement income.

Estimated Retirement Income and Expenses Worksheet

1. Total annual retirement income:
company pension   _____
CPP/QPP   _____
part-time employment   _____
other (i.e. rental income) _____

Total 1 (value today) $_____

Total 2 (estimated value at retirement) $_____

2. Investment and Savings — When you retire, chances are you'll draw on most or all of your savings and investments. To determine how much annual income you may be able to generate from your investments and savings during retirement (Total 4), enlist the help of financial software, financial Web sites or a financial advisor.

all RRSPs   _____
other investments   _____
savings   _____

Total 3 (value today) $_____

Total 4 (estimated annual income
Total 3 will generate when you retire) $_____

3. Estimated Annual Expenses — Base your answers on what these items cost today. Once you've totaled all your expenses and have entered the figure in the space provided for Total 5, again use financial software or financial Web sites, or consult a financial advisor, to project what retirement expenses will be. Then enter the figure in the space provided for Total 6.

housing (mortgage or rent, if applicable) _____
  property taxes   _____
  utilities   _____
  maintenance   _____
  improvements   _____

furniture, appliances   _____
food   _____
clothing   _____
transportation   _____
  car payments   _____
  gas   _____
  maintenance   _____
  taxi fare   _____
  public transportation   _____
insurance   _____
  vehicle   _____
  property   _____
  liability   _____
  other   _____
medical and dental care   _____
entertainment   _____
  dining out   _____
  movies, theatre, sports events, etc.   _____
  hobbies   _____
vacations   _____
income tax   _____
gifts   _____
charitable giving   _____
other   _____

Total 5 (cost today) $_____

Total 6 (estimated costs
when you retire) $_____

**Part 4. Total estimated annual
retirement income less
total projected annual expenses**
(add Totals 2 and 4,
and subtract Total 6): $_____

Putting it all together

Treat your financial plan as a work in progress.

It's a continual process

Having come this far puts you well ahead of the vast majority of Canadians who merely dream about financial security. By reading this book you've taken the initiative to learn about net worth, different investments, insurance, income tax, helping your kids with their education, retirement planning, and many other important topics. But the journey doesn't stop here.

As we've pointed out, your financial plan is a living document, one that you must review in detail at least once a year. If there's a big change in your life, such as a promotion or having a relative move in with you for a while, you'll need to re-examine how this change affects your financial circumstances now and into the future. Regularly assessing your financial health will let you measure how well you're doing and give you time to make adjustments. And whenever you do your review, allow adequate time and ensure your surroundings are tranquil. Even if this means farming out the kids to a relative on a Saturday afternoon, your reward will outweigh the effort.

Calculate your personal net worth growth

In reviewing your plan, one key task is to see how far you've come from the previous year. To do this, subtract last year's net worth (chapter 1) from this year's and calculate the difference as a percentage of last year's figure. If your net worth last year was $200,000 and this year it's $240,000, your net worth has grown by 20% ($40,000 = 20% of $200,000). If you're calculating the percentage manually, you'd do it as follows:

$$\frac{(\$240,000 - \$200,000) \times 100}{\$200,000}$$

$$= \frac{\$40,000 \times 100}{\$200,000}$$

$$= 20\%$$

A 20% annual return on your net worth is what many financial planners suggest. However, if your goals are very costly or you don't have many years to amass your nest egg, you'll likely need a higher annual return, plus some sound strategies to help you to get there. You should also realize that your net worth might stay flat or even decrease, perhaps due to a setback like a salary cut. If this happens, adjust your plan as soon as the change occurs. Similarly, if you come into money unexpectedly, put it to work for you right away.

Stay informed

Between your regular financial checkups, it's important to read the financial pages regularly — daily if you can. There always seems to be something on the horizon, whether it's recommendations from a parliamentary committee, changes to RRSP contribution rules, or new tax laws. Many changes that can affect your family's finances are announced in the federal budget which is delivered in February. It's also wise to keep abreast of any mini budgets, plus the budget delivered in your province each year. These changes may affect your plan and your strategies. And however you put your money to work, keep regular tabs on your investments and the economy. Many financial firms include newsletters with client statements, and you might pick up some good tips.

Finding a financial advisor

Taking good care of your financial well-being demands a lot of time and know-how. If you lack one or both of these commodities, don't despair. Financial professionals abound in even the smallest communities. These people may bill themselves as financial advisors or specialists, investment advisors, stock brokers, mutual fund specialists, insurance salespeople, accountants, tax specialists, lawyers — or use other titles. Eager to make themselves known, financial professionals often advertise, write columns in the local paper, or host seminars for the general public.

A good place to start your search is to ask friends, colleagues and relatives if they've dealt with an advisor. Then find what advice and service was provided, how long your friend has known the professional, and the level of satisfaction. Once you've got a short list, call each one and ask pointed questions about their areas of expertise, how long they've been in that business, what products they sell, how they're paid and the professional qualifications they hold. At the end of this chapter, you'll find a summary of the main financial designations, their granting organizations, and the requirements.

Of course, don't simply take any designation at face value. Ask what the designation stands for, what the advisor did to get it, and who offers it. Sometimes when a designation is introduced, changed or replaced, the sponsoring organization will have relaxed rules to get the credential off the ground. This is called grandfathering. Don't be shy about asking a professional how they obtained their designation. And if you think an advisor may not hold the designation he claims, call the issuing organization. These organizations have reputations to protect, and want to ensure that everyone using their designation is in good standing.

You may need different specialists

If you decide to use a financial advisor, you may also need to consult specialized professionals. An accountant, for example, can help you wade through complex tax matters and offer tax-saving strategies particular to your circumstances. A generalist, on the other hand, should recognize what falls within their professional capacity and indicate when more specialized advice is needed.

Understanding financial designations

Professionals in many disciplines often include their designations on their business cards and letterhead. But what do these strings of letters after their names really mean? The information below is designed to help unravel the mystery.

CA (Chartered Accountant)
Granted by: provincial institutes of chartered accountants.
Requirements: Specific education and experience,

and successful completion of the rigorous Uniform Final Examination (UFE). Must adhere to a code of professional/ethical conduct.

CFA (Chartered Financial Analyst)
Granted by: Association for Investment Management and Research.
Requirements: Held mainly by institutional money managers and stock analysts, candidates must pass rigorous exams.

CFP (Certified Financial Planner)
Granted by: Financial Planners Standards Council of Canada
Requirements: Meet or exceed a uniform set of standards of core and continuing education, two or more years' experience, professional conduct and agreement to report infractions to the council.

CGA (Certified General Accountant)
Granted by: provincial associations of certified general accountants.
Requirements: Successful completion of specific education and exams, plus experience and professional/ethical conduct.

CIM (Certified Investment Manager)
Granted by: Canadian Securities Institute.
Requirements: Completion of the Canadian Investment Management program. Leads to licensing as a portfolio manager.

CLU (Chartered Life Underwriter)

Granted by: Canadian Association of Insurance and Financial Advisors.

Requirements: Successful completion of a series of exams, indicating the candidate's competence as a qualified life insurance agent.

CMA (Certified Management Accountant)

Granted by: provincial societies of management accountants.

Requirements: Successful completion of educational courses and exams, experience and professional/ethical conduct.

FCA (Fellow of the Institute of Chartered Accountants)

Granted by: provincial institutes of chartered accountants.

Requirements: Membership in a provincial institute of chartered accountants, prescribed standards of career excellence and achievement, plus professional and community contribution.

FCGA (Fellow of the Certified General Accountants' Association)

Granted by: provincial associations of certified general accountants.

Requirements: Membership in a provincial association of certified general accountants, prescribed standards of career excellence and achievement, plus professional and community contributions.

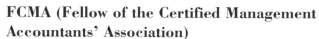

FCMA (Fellow of the Certified Management Accountants' Association)

Granted by: Certified Management Accountants' Association (CMAA).

Requirements: CMAA membership, plus prescribed standards of excellence in career achievement, plus professional and community contributions.

FCSI (Fellow of the Canadian Securities Institute)

Granted by: Canadian Securities Institute.

Requirements: High-level educational requirements, at least five years' experience, ethical conduct and commitment to continuing professional education.

FMA (Financial Management Advisor)

Granted by: Canadian Securities Institute

Requirements: Completion of the financial management stream which includes courses in professional financial planning and wealth management.

Appendix

Financial websites

If you're connected to the Internet, you've got access to all kinds of financial information. But you might want some help sorting out the useful information from the myriad of sites.

Staff of the Investor Learning Centre of Canada's resource centres in Toronto and Calgary have compiled the following select list of financial, investment and retirement-related web sites. They've used their expertise and professional judgement to check the sites for comprehensiveness, content, analysis, ease of use, editorial content and timeliness.

Sites that contain Canadian information are indicated by a ✺. Bilingual sites are marked by the ⚜. As well, sites we consider to be particularly comprehensive get two stars. Don't forget to check out the Investor Learning Centre's own website at **www.investorlearning.ca**

Remember to type the site "address" exactly as listed. Some sites track useage by asking you for a password. Don't confuse the need to register and provide a password with the necessity to become a subscriber. Some sites offer a limited amount of information for free and require you to register and pay a fee before you can access more detailed information.

Banking

✺ ⚜ Canadian Bankers Association —
http://www.cba.ca
Comprehensive information about the banking industry. Information booklets available on-line or through the mail.

Government Sources

♣ ⚜ Bank of Canada —
http://www.bank-banque-canada.ca
Includes recent publications (press releases &
speeches), current market rates, exchange rates and
more.

♣ ⚜ Canadian Deposit Insurance Corporation —
http://www.cdic.ca
A federal crown corporation created in 1967 to protect
the money deposited in financial institutions that are
CDIC members. The site explains how deposit
insurance works.

♣ ⚜ Canadian Investment and Savings —
http://www.cis-pec.gc.ca
Government of Canada securities information.

♣ ⚜ Government of Canada: intergovernmental links —
http://www.intergov.gc.ca
Links to municipal, provincial, federal and
international government agencies that use on-line and
information technologies to improve the access and
delivery of government services to the public.
Searchable.

♣ ⚜ Revenue Canada — http://www.rc.gc.ca
**Comprehensive coverage of the tax rules. General
tax information, forms, FAQs, contacts, news and more.

🍁 ⚜ Statistics Canada —
http://www.statcan.ca/start.html
**Access to Statistics Canada data, some free, news of statistical releases, and analysis. Links.

🍁 ⚜ Strategis from Industry Canada —
http://strategis.ic.gc.ca
** Information and analysis of interest to business and investors. Check out the consumer affairs pages.

Insurance

🍁 Insurance Canada — **http://www.insurance-canada.ca**
** Helpful articles and resources on insurance with extensive links to other consumer sites.

🍁 Term4Sale —
http://www.term4sale.com/T4SALECA/termsale.htm
*** Site that lets you compare term insurance rates from a number of Canadian insurers by inputting your personal information.

🍁 Canadian Association of Insurance and Financial Advisors — **http://www.caifa.com**
CAIFA provides information on financial service matters to consumers and the media on choosing a financial advisor, how RRIF's and annuities work, RRSP rules, RESP's, life insurance, speeches and biographies of industry leaders.

Investment Organizations

🍁 ⚜ Canadian Association of Financial Planners —
http://www.cafp.org
Information about the role of the financial planner.
FAQs.

🍁 ⚜ Canadian Investor Protection Fund (CIPF) —
http://www.cipf.ca
Details about financial protection available to
consumers who deal with CIPF members. List of
members.

🍁 ⚜ Canadian Securities Institute —
http://www.csi.ca
Information about training programs for securities
industry and financial service professionals, also
available to interested individuals. On-line registration.

🍁 ⚜ Investor Learning Centre of Canada —
http://www.investorlearning.ca
Contains an investment terms glossary and online
versions of Investment Facts brochures, a bookstore
and virtual library, investment FAQ's, an on-line
investment education course and a review of
investment links. French site under construction.

Investor services

🍁 ⚜ Carlson On-line Services —
http://www.carlsononline.com
Canadian investor relations information - the site that
brings it altogether. Includes info on 4,000 Canadian
companies, press releases from the major newswires,

website links, stock quotes, charting and insider trading.

❦ Financial Services Network — **http://www.fsn.ca**
Independent Canadian financial services site. Comprehensive list of Canadian financial services firms. Borrowing and savings rates, mortgage and savings calculators.

❦ I*Money — **http://www.imoney.com**
Canada's personal finance website providing timely quotes, investment library, discussion forum and investment tools.

❦ ⚜ Quicken Financial Network — **http://www.quicken.ca**
**A comprehensive Canadian tax and investment site. Free data and analysis, commentary, investor tools and interactivity. A full-service financial site.

❦ ⚜ Yahoo! Canada — **http://www.yahoo.ca**
** Extensive financial tools for free with links to other useful Canadian sites.

❦ BigCharts — **http://www.bigchartscanada.com**
Free technical charts and other information for stock market investors.

Mutual funds
❦ Fund Counsel — **http://www.fundcounsel.com**
The site includes some free information on mutual fund companies and investment strategies. Best of all is a

"Battle of the Funds" comparison.

🍁 The Fund Library — **http://www.fundlib.com**
**A comprehensive mutual fund resource centre
providing company information, a personal fund
monitor and portfolio tracker, a discussion forum and
learning centre.

🍁 Globefund — **http://www.globefund.com**
**Provides reliable up-to-date and unbiased
information, combines the Globe and Mail's mutual
fund data with published articles from financial
journalists, profiles of funds and companies and a
learning section for novice investors.

News organizations and publications
🍁 Canoe (Canadian Online Explorer) —
http://www.canoe.ca
Sun Media and related publications online, plus a
useful money section.

🍁 Financial Post -
http://www.nationalpost.com/financialpost.asp
Highlights from current FP; follow mutual funds;
search by exchange and industry, etc.

🍁 Globe and Mail —
http://www.theglobeandmail.com
Current news, including Report on Business. Closing
quotes.

Retirement Planning

🍁 Retire Canada —
http://retirecanada.miningco.com
A Canadian site offering links to all types of retirement planning information.

🍁 RetireWeb — **http://www.retireweb.com**
Financial information to help with all stages of retirement planning. Includes calculators for various investment vehicles. A Canadian site.

Taxation

🍁 ⚜ Canadian Tax Foundation — **http://www.ctf.ca**
CTF researches tax issues to aid public policy development. Very useful links.

🍁 Ernst & Young (Canada) —
http://www.eycan.com
Canadian and provincial tax calculators, budget information, answers to tax questions submitted to E&Y, links and more.

🍁 ⚜ Jacks on Tax — **http://www.jackstax.com**
Well-known author of books about taxation. Website includes selected info. and tax tip of the week.

🍁 ⚜ KPMG (Canada) — **http://www.kpmg.ca**

🍁 ⚜ Revenue Canada — **http://www.rc.gc.ca**
Comprehensive coverage of the tax rules. General tax information, forms, FAQs, contacts, news and more.

Women and Investing

Equity — http://www.equitymag.com
A magazine about women and money. (American).

Independent Means —
http://www.anincomeofherown.com
Targeted at girls under 20, it focuses on
entrepreneurial skills, making money and mentoring.
Featured categories are website links for teens, careers,
business, women's issues and resources.

❀ Women and Retirement —
http://retirecanada.miningco.com
Includes demographic information as well as articles
on poverty, pension reform, investing and financial
planning as it applies to Canadian women.

Women and Finance —
http://womenswire.com/money
Includes all aspects of investing. American site.

Young Investors

❀ ⚜ CIBC's Smart Start Youth Site —
http://www.cibc.com/smartstart
There are lots of games, and activities as well as tips
and information on money and banking, as well as
mascot "Flip" The Coin.

KidsBank.Com — http://www.kidsbank.com
US bank website that explains the fundamentals of
money and banking to children.

Investing for Kids —
http://tqd.advanced.org/3096/index.htm
Designed by kids for kids, it examines stocks, bonds,
mutual funds and the like.

It teaches the principles of saving and investing. It
also includes a stock game, a quiz, and a glossary.

YoungBiz.com — **http://www.youngbiz.com**
An entrepreneurial Web site that teaches kids how to
use skills they already have to make good financial
decisions. A daily market update offers quotes and
news.

Young Investor — **http://www.younginvestor.com**
Teaches the basic concepts of investing through
character guides, a library and dictionary of financial
terms.

Not-for-profit
credit counselling agencies

These organizations offer you a range of credit counselling services

British Columbia
Credit Counselling Society of B.C.
Toll Free: 1-888-527-8999
(only in B.C.)
Tel: 604-527-8999
Fax: 604-527-8008

Debtor Assistance Branch
Ministry of Attorney General
Toll Free: 1-800-663-7867 (only in B.C.)
Victoria:
Tel: 250-387-1747
Fax: 250-953-4783
Burnaby:
Tel: 604-660-3550
Fax: 604-660-8472
Kamloops:
Tel: 250-828-4511
Fax: 250-371-3822

Alberta
Credit Counselling Services of Alberta
Toll Free: 1-888-294-0076
(only in Alberta)
Calgary:
Tel: 403-265-2201
Fax: 403-265-2240

Edmonton:
Tel: 780-423-5265
Fax: 780-423-2791

Saskatchewan
Department of Justice, Provincial Mediation Board
Regina:
Tel: 306-787-5387
Fax: 306-787-5574
Saskatoon:
Tel: 306-933-6520
Fax: 306-933-7030

Manitoba
Community Financial Counselling Services
Tel: 204-989-1900
Fax: 204-989-1908

Ontario
Ontario Association of Credit Counselling Services
Toll Free:1-888-746-3328
Fax: 905-945-4680

Quebec
Féderation des associations coopératives de'économie
familiale du Québec
Tel: 514-271-7004
Fax: 514-271-1036

Option-consommateurs
Tel: 514-598-7288
Fax: 514-598-8511

Newfoundland & Labrador
Personal Credit Counselling Service
Tel: 709-753-5812
Fax: 709-753-3390

Prince Edward Island
Department of Community Affairs
Consumer, Corporate and Insurance Services
Tel: 902-368-4580
Fax: 902-368-5355

Nova Scotia
Port Cities Debt Counselling Society
Tel: 902-453-6510
Access Nova Scotia
Department of Business and Consumer Services
Toll Free: 1-800-670-4357 (only in Nova Scotia)
Fax: 902-424-0720

New Brunswick
Credit Counselling Services of Atlantic Canada, Inc.
Toll Free:1-800-539-2227 (only in New Brunswick)
Tel: 506-652-1613
Fax: 506-633-6057

Consumers Services Officer
Consumer Affairs Branch,
Department of Justice
Tel: 506-453-2659
Fax: 506-444-4494
Family Enrichment and Counselling Services
Tel: 506-458-8211
Fax: 506-451-9437

Yukon

For a referral, contact: Consumer Services,
Department of Justice
Tel: 867-667-5111
Fax: 867-667-3609

Northwest Territories

Consumer Services
Municipal and Community Affairs
Tel: 867-873-7125
Fax: 867-920-6343

Calculate your mortgage payment
blended payment of principal and interest* per $1,000 of loan. If the amortization period is **15 years...**

Rate*	Monthly payment	Semi-monthly payment	Bi-weekly	Weekly payment
5.00%	5.816	2.905	2.678	1.338
5.25%	5.959	2.976	2.743	1.371
5.50%	6.104	3.049	2.810	1.404
5.75%	6.250	3.121	2.877	1.438
6.00%	6.398	3.195	2.944	1.471
6.25%	6.547	3.270	3.013	1.506
6.50%	6.698	3.345	3.082	1.540
6.75%	6.851	3.421	3.152	1.575
7.00%	7.004	3.497	3.222	1.610
7.25%	7.159	3.574	3.293	1.645
7.50%	7.316	3.652	3.365	1.681
7.75%	7.473	3.731	3.437	1.717
8.00%	7.632	3.810	3.510	1.754
8.25%	7.792	3.890	3.583	1.790
8.50%	7.954	3.970	3.657	1.827
8.75%	8.116	4.051	3.731	1.864
9.00%	8.280	4.132	3.806	1.902
9.25%	8.444	4.214	3.882	1.939
9.50%	8.610	4.297	3.958	1.977
9.75%	8.777	4.380	4.034	2.015
10.00%	8.945	4.463	4.111	2.053
10.25%	9.114	4.547	4.188	2.092
10.50%	9.283	4.632	4.266	2.131
10.75%	9.454	4.717	4.344	2.170
11.00%	9.625	4.802	4.422	2.209

Interest calculated half-yearly, not in advance.

213

Calculate your mortgage payment

blended payment of principal and interest* per $1,000 of loan. If the amortization period is **25 years...**

Rate*	Monthly payment	Semi-monthly payment	Bi-weekly	Weekly payment
5.00%	7.881	3.937	3.630	1.814
5.25%	8.009	4.000	3.689	1.843
5.50%	8.138	4.064	3.748	1.873
5.75%	8.268	4.129	3.807	1.903
6.00%	8.399	4.194	3.867	1.933
6.25%	8.531	4.260	3.928	1.963
6.50%	8.664	4.326	3.988	1.993
6.75%	8.789	4.393	4.050	2.024
7.00%	8.932	4.460	4.111	2.054
7.25%	9.068	4.527	4.174	2.085
7.50%	9.205	4.596	4.236	2.117
7.75%	9.343	4.664	4.299	2.148
8.00%	9.482	4.733	4.363	2.180
8.25%	9.621	4.802	4.427	2.212
8.50%	9.762	4.872	4.491	2.244
8.75%	9.903	4.943	4.555	2.276
9.00%	10.045	5.013	4.620	2.308
9.25%	10.188	5.085	4.686	2.341
9.50%	10.332	5.156	4.752	2.374
9.75%	10.477	5.228	4.818	2.407
10.00%	10.623	5.301	4.885	2.440
10.25%	10.769	5.373	4.951	2.473
10.50%	10.916	5.447	5.019	2.507
10.75%	11.064	5.520	5.086	2.541
11.00%	11.213	5.594	5.154	2.575

Interest calculated half-yearly, not in advance.

Glossary

Glossary

Accidental death and dismemberment benefit: Insurance paid if you die accidentally or lose one or more body parts, such as an arm or an eye.

Accidental death benefit: When a life insurance benefit doubles or triples if the death is accidental.

Accumulation plan: An arrangement that lets you buy mutual fund shares regularly in small or large amounts.

Adjusted cost base: The original purchase price of an asset plus any acquisition costs, such as commission or fees.

All Risk Coverage: Property insurance that only excludes coverage for specifically mentioned items.

Amortization: The number of years it will take to pay off your mortgage.

Annuitant: A person who buys an annuity and will get payments from it.

Annuity: A contract that guarantees you a series of payments in exchange for your lump sum investment. Life annuities pay for your lifetime and fixed-term annuities until you reach age 90.

Attribution rules: When investment income is earned by one person but taxed in the hands of the previous owner.

Average tax rate: Less than your marginal tax rate, this is your total tax bill calculated as a percentage of your taxable income. If you pay $15,000 on $60,000 taxable income, then your average tax rate is 25%.

Back-end load: A sales commission charged when you sell mutual fund units. Usually starts at 6% to 8% in year one and declines to zero in six to eight years. Most often you have a choice between a back-end load or a front-end load, though some funds charge both.

Balanced fund: A mutual fund that holds a combination of stocks, bonds and cash; usually managed to fit the needs of conservative investors.

Bank Rate: The rate at which the Bank of Canada makes short-term loans to chartered banks and other financial institutions, and the benchmark for prime rates set by financial institutions.

Basis Point: One basis point equals one-hundredth of one per cent.

Bear market: A falling stock market.

Beneficiary: The person entitled to the proceeds of a life insurance policy or registered account when you die.

Blue chip: A descriptive term usually applied to high grade stocks.

Book value: The purchase price of an investment plus reinvested income; used to calculate foreign content in an RRSP or other registered plan.

Bond: A long-term investment that can be bought or sold in the bond market and which pays annual interest in semi-annual installments until a future maturity date when the bond's face value is paid to the holder.

Bond fund: A mutual fund that holds mainly bonds and other fixed-income investments such as debentures and mortgage-backed securities.

Broker: A person who charges commission to handle your orders to buy and sell investments or other property.

Bull market: A rising stock market.

Canada Pension Plan (CPP): A federal social security program that pays monthly pensions to contributors, their surviving spouses or orphaned children. Also may be paid if you are disabled.

Canada Savings Bond: A bond issued each year by the federal government, can be cashed at any time for full face value.

Capital: Typically, the money or property used in a business; also refers to cash in reserve or savings.

Capital gain: The sale price of an asset less its adjusted cost base and any selling costs.

Capital gain exemption: An exemption from capital gains tax on qualified small business and farm property as defined by Revenue Canada.

Capital gains tax: Tax paid at your marginal rate on 75% of any

capital gain realized in the year.

Capital loss: The loss resulting from selling an investment for less than you paid; can be applied against any capital gains in the past three years or may be carried forward indefinitely.

Cash equivalent: Any investment that can be quickly converted to cash with little risk of losing part of your principal.

Cash flow: How much money you have coming in compared to how much you're spending.

Cash surrender value: The amount you get by agreeing to surrender a life insurance policy.

Child tax benefit: A refundable tax credit paid monthly to low- and middle-income families with children.

Closed mortgage: A mortgage that puts limits on your right to pay it off before the term is up.

Claw-back: Commonly applied to Old Age Security and Employment Insurance, an amount you have to repay based on your income level.

Closed-end fund: An investment fund company that issues a fixed number of shares which aren't redeemable, but instead are bought and sold on stock exchanges.

Codicil: An update or change to a will prepared by a lawyer and properly witnessed.

Commercial paper: Short-term negotiable debt issued by non-financial corporations with a term of a few days to a year.

Common stock: An investment representing part-ownership of a company.

Compounding: The process where income is earned on income.

Consumer price index: A reading on the inflation rate because it shows the rise or fall in the cost of living for consumers.

Contractual plan: An agreement to buy a set amount of mutual fund units at specified times.

Convertible mortgage: An open mortgage that gives you the right to later lock in a set interest rate, if you choose.

Convertible term: Term life insurance that you can, within certain time limits, convert to a permanent or whole life policy without having to provide satisfactory medical information.

Coupon rate: A bond's annual interest rate.

Custodian: A bank, trust or other financial institution that holds a mutual fund's securities and cash in safekeeping.

Death benefit: A payment from life insurance made by the insurance company if the insured person dies.

Debenture: A bond unsecured by any pledge of property. It is supported by the general credit of the issuing corporation.

Decreasing term: Life insurance where the premium stays constant but where the benefits are reduced monthly or annually.

Deferred annuity: An annuity bought with a monthly or a lump-sum amount where payments begin after a number of years or at a specified age.

Deferral: Postponing tax on income to future years by deducting contributions to an RRSP from your earned income and letting income from investments accumulate tax-sheltered in the plan. The main benefit is that you will be in a lower tax bracket when you withdraw and pay tax on the money.

Deferred profit sharing plan: A retirement savings plan where your employer shares profits with non-shareholder employees for retirement. Contributions are tax-deductible for the company and tax-sheltered until you withdraw them from the plan.

Defined benefit pension plan: A registered pension plan guaranteeing a specific income at retirement, based on earnings and number of years worked.

Defined contribution pension plan: A registered pension plan that does not promise you a specified benefit at retirement, but which depends on the returns of the investments in which you choose to invest your and any company contributions.

Distributions: Payments to investors by a mutual fund from interest or dividend income or from selling securities at a profit.

Diversification: Spreading investments over a variety of asset types, industries or geographic areas to reduce risk.

Dividend: A per-share payment out of company profits, paid to shareholders.

Dividend fund: A mutual fund that generally invests in preferred shares or common shares of senior corporations with a history of regular dividend payments.

Dividend tax credit: An income tax credit gives you a tax break on dividend income from shares of Canadian corporations.

Dollar cost averaging: When you regularly invest equal amounts thereby automatically buying more units or shares when prices are low and fewer when prices are high; can reduce your average cost per share.

Earned income: For tax purposes, earned income is generally employment income and some taxable benefits. It is used to calculate your maximum RRSP contribution.

Employee Stock Purchase Plan (ESPP): An employer-sponsored plan that lets you buy the company's stock at a discount to its market value.

Equity fund: A mutual fund that invests mainly in common stocks.

Employment Insurance (EI): A government plan that temporarily pays a limited income to you if you become unemployed, or if you are on maternity or parental leave.

Estate: Your estate consists of everything you own at the time of your death, including real estate, investments and personal effects.

Executor: The person who has the power to distribute the assets in your estate according to the instructions in your will.

Face value: The amount that will be paid to the holder when a debt security, such as a bond, matures. Also called the principal amount, par value or denomination.

Fair market value: Used to determine the value of investments transferred into an RRSP, this is the price a willing buyer would pay a willing seller if neither was under any compulsion to buy or sell.

Fiduciary: An individual or institution holding a position of trust, including an executor, administrator or trustee.

Financial planning: Taking charge of your financial affairs so you can make the best use of your money resources.

Fixed-dollar withdrawal plan: A plan that gives you a fixed-dollar payment monthly or quarterly out of a mutual fund at set intervals.

Fixed-income investments: Investments like bonds that produce a fixed amount of income that usually does not vary over the life of the investment.

Fixed-period withdrawal plan: A withdrawal plan designed to deplete your mutual fund holdings over a set period.

Fixed-Term annuity: Gives you periodic payments of equal amounts for a fixed period, e.g. 5, 10, or 20 years.

Front-end load: A sales commission - usually 4% to 5% of your investment, but negotiable -- charged when you buy mutual fund units. While less popular with investors, front-end loads are generally regarded as the better load option because of lower ongoing management expenses and better flexibility.

Growth stocks: Shares of companies with earnings that are expected to increase at a greater rate than the overall market.

Guaranteed Income Supplement (GIS): A pension for Old Age Security (OAS) recipients who have little or no other income source.

Guaranteed investment certificates: A deposit-type investment offered by banks, trust companies and other financial institutions which pays a predetermined interest rate for a specified period.

Guaranteed term annuity: An annuity where payments are guaranteed for a specific length of time, and where payments continue to the beneficiary if you die before the term ends.

Guardianship: Used in a will to decide who will care for a child if the parents die; usually includes alternate guardians should the designated guardian be unable to fulfil the role.

Home equity loan: A line of credit secured by your home which usually carries a lower interest rate than other types of loans.

Income funds: Mutual funds that invest mainly in fixed-income securities like bonds, mortgages and preferred shares.

Income splitting: Distribution taxable income from an individual in a high tax-bracket to one in a lower tax bracket to reduce overall taxes paid.

Index fund: A mutual fund that holds - either directly or indirectly through derivative instruments -- the same kinds of investments that make up a stock index or other financial market index to match the market's general returns.

Inflation: When prices are generally rising; commonly measured by the Consumer Price Index.

Insurance deductible: The portion of a loss that you must pay before insurance is paid.

Insurance riders: Conditions attached to an insurance policy that either expand, reduce or waive the basic coverage.

Interest: What it costs to borrow or "rent" other people's money.

International fund: A mutual fund that holds investments from the world's major economies excluding North America.

Intestate: When you die without leaving a will and the government decides what will become of your assets and who would look after any orphaned children.

Investment advisor: An individual licensed to provide advice on a wide range of investments, including stocks, bonds and mutual funds.

Investment counsel: An individual or a firm that provides investment advice to wealthy individuals and pension and mutual funds, generally for a percentage of the assets invested.

Investment representative: A person similarly qualified to an investment advisor, but who works for a discount brokerage and is not permitted to offer specific investment advice.

Investment dealer: A brokerage firm.

Joint and last survivor: An annuity that pays benefits until both you and your spouse die.

Lease: A contract that gives you use of a car, real estate or equipment for a specified period.

Leverage: Using borrowed money to invest; cost of the borrowed money needs to be less than returns on the investment in order to be successful.

Life Income Fund (LIF): An investment account created to access locked-in RRSP and pension plan savings for income in retirement.

Liability insurance: Protects you if you hurt someone in a car accident or if a person slips and falls on your porch.

Life annuity: An annuity where payments are guaranteed for the life of the person who holds the annuity.

Life expectancy adjusted withdrawal plan: A plan where your holdings in a mutual fund are depleted while giving maximum income over your lifetime.

Line of credit: An agreement negotiated between a borrower and a lender establishing the maximum amount of money a borrower may draw. The agreement also sets out other conditions, e.g., how and when money is to be repaid.

Liquidity: Refers to the ease with which an investment may be converted to cash at a reasonable price.

Living will: Living wills express a person's wishes about the kind of medical treatment they wish, or do not wish, to receive when they are not able to make decisions for themselves. Living wills are not binding in all provinces.

Locked-In Retirement Account: An account in which locked-in funds from a registered pension plan are deposited before being transferred to a LIF at or before age 69.

Loads: Sales commissions levied on holders of mutual fund units.

Lump-sum distribution: A payment of all your retirement money when you leave a company or when you retire. Distributions prior to retirement are usually rolled over into other retirement plans or into a locked-in RRSP.

Management expense ratio: The amount spent on the management and operation of a mutual fund, expressed as a percentage of the fund's average net assets. It includes management fees, transfer agent expenses, custodial fees, and

other direct operating expenses, but excludes brokerage commissions, taxes, or interest charges.

Management fee: The money paid to the mutual fund to manage the investment portfolio.

Marginal tax rate: The rate of tax you pay on your last dollar of taxable income.

Market index: A vehicle used to denote trends in securities markets. The best known in Canada is the Toronto Stock Exchange 300 Composite Index (TSE 300).

Maturity: The date a bond or debenture comes due and must be redeemed or paid off.

Money market: Part of the capital market where short-term securities like treasury bills are bought and sold.

Money market fund: A mutual fund that invests mainly in treasury bills and other short-term investments.

Money purchase pension plan: Same as a defined contribution pension plan.

Mortgage fund: A mutual fund that holds mortgages, typically first mortgages on residential property.

Mortgage-backed securities: An investment representing ownership in a pool of mortgages that generate regular payments of principal and interest; usually sold in blocks of $5,000.

Net asset value: The value of all investments in a mutual fund, minus the fund's liabilities.

Net asset value per share or NAVPS: A mutual fund's net asset value divided by the number of units outstanding to give you each unit's value.

Net worth: The difference between the total value of your assets and your liabilities.

No-load fund: A mutual fund that doesn't charge a sales commission to buy or sell its shares.

Notary: In Quebec, a notary is an office lawyer as opposed to a trial lawyer.

Old Age Security (OAS): A pension payable to everyone who is

65 or older, meets an income needs test and is resident in Canada.

Open mortgage: A mortgage that lets you make extra payments or pay off the whole balance without any penalties.

Open-end fund: An investment fund that issues and redeems units on an ongoing basis; most mutual funds are open-ended.

Overcontribution Allowance for RRSP: A lifetime $2,000 permitted contribution to an RRSP above your contribution limit. While not deductible from taxable income, the overcontribution grows tax-free.

Pension adjustment: An amount that reduces how much you are allowed to contribute to your RRSP, based on benefits you've earned from your company pension or deferred profit sharing plan.

Pension Adjustment Reversal (PAR): An adjustment to regain lost RRSP contribution room due to previous pension adjustments for people who left pension plans after January 1, 1997.

Pension plan: A formal arrangement through which the employer, and in most cases the employee, contribute to a fund to provide the employee with a lifetime income after retirement.

Pension portability: The ability to switch one company's pension plan benefits to another company's plan or your own locked-in account when you change jobs.

Permanent life insurance: Life insurance coverage that typically covers you for life, and has a savings feature known as the cash surrender value.

Portfolio: All the investments that a mutual fund or an individual investor owns.

Posted rate: The regular interest rate charged for a mortgage; if you negotiate you might get a better deal.

Power of attorney: Special authority you can give to another person to make financial or personal care decisions on your behalf.

Pre-approved mortgage: Where you know much you can spend on that house because you've already lined up the money from your financial institution.

Pre-payment option: A feature of many mortgages that lets you increase or double up your payments

Preferred share: Part ownership in a company, with a claim on dividends - and on assets if company is liquidated - ahead of common shareholders.

Present value: The current worth of an amount to be received in the future. In the case of an annuity, present value is the current worth of a series of equal payments to be made in the future.

Principal: Your capital; the par value of a bond.

Prime rate: The rate of interest banks charge their most creditworthy business customers on short-term loans; used as a guide for other customers.

Prospectus: A legal document in which the investment objectives and risks of a mutual fund or other security are disclosed to the public.

Ratio withdrawal plan: A mutual fund withdrawal plan giving investors income based on a percentage of the value of units held.

Real estate fund: A mutual fund that invests primarily in residential and/or commercial real estate to produce income and capital gains for its unitholders.

Real estate investment trust (REIT): A closed-end investment company holding real estate or mortgage investments.

Rebalance: Adjusting the proportion of stocks, bonds or other investment types to bring the portfolio back to the desired asset allocation.

Registered Education Savings Plan (RESP): A plan that lets you accumulate tax deferred savings to most often pay for a child's post-secondary education.

Registered Pension Plan (RPP): A private pension plan often set up by your employer; may be either defined benefit or defined contribution.

Registered Retirement Income Fund (RRIF): An option for collapsing your RRSP at retirement that gives you continued tax-sheltered growth and investment flexibility while also requiring minimum annual withdrawals.

Registered Retirement Savings Plan (RRSP): A retirement

plan that lets you get a tax deduction on your contributions, and shelter from tax the growth on the investments in the plan.

Retiring allowance: An amount you may get from an employer when you retire after long service.

Reserve: A whole life insurance feature that gives you options for such things as buying an annuity for retirement income or to stop premium payments.

Rollover: Transferring money from one registered pension or retirement plan to another without triggering taxes when you change jobs.

Sales charges: Fees you pay on mutual funds either when you buy or when you sell - and sometimes both - calculated as a percentage of the amount invested or withdrawn.

Self-directed RRSP: An RRSP account in which you can buy and sell a wider variety of investments such as stocks, bonds and mutual funds.

Segregated funds: Investment funds that guarantee to return at least three quarters of your original investment at maturity - usually 10 years -- or on your death.

Simplified prospectus: Used in the sale of mutual funds, this is a simplified version of the full prospectus, a legal document that tells you about the fund's investment objectives, risks, fees and other important topics.

Small cap stock: Shares of a small company where the value of all shares owned by investors is less than $500 million; often recommended for long-term investment due to their high short-term volatility.

Spousal RRSP: An RRSP account controlled by one spouse but to which the other spouse contributes and claims a tax deduction. Used to balance the income that each spouse receives in retirement to cut their combined tax burden.

Strip bonds: A highly volatile bond that does not pay you interest but which is sold at a discount to its future maturity value. The gain at maturity is calculated as an annual percentage return and is taxable each year as interest.

Systematic withdrawal plan: Plans offered by mutual fund companies that allow unitholders to receive payment from their investment at regular intervals.

Tax credit: An income tax credit that directly reduces the amount of income tax you pay by offsetting other income tax liabilities.

Tax deduction: A reduction of total income before the amount of income tax payable is calculated.

Tax shelter: An investment that may reduce or delay payment of taxes.

Term insurance: Temporary life insurance that covers the policyholder for a specific time.

Term to 90 annuity: An annuity that pays a fixed amount each year until it is exhausted in the year that the annuitant turns 90.

Treasury bill (T-bill): Short-term government debt. Treasury bills bear no interest, but are sold at a discount. The difference between the discount price and par value is the return to be received by the investor.

Trust: An instrument placing ownership of property in the name of one person, called a trustee, to be held by the trustee for the use and benefit of some other person.

Umbrella insurance: Extra add-on liability insurance.

Universal life insurance: A life insurance term policy that is renewed each year and which has both an insurance component and an investment component. The investment component invests excess premiums and generates returns to the policyholder.

Variable life annuity: An annuity providing a fluctuating level of payments, depending on the performance of its underlying investments.

Vesting: In pension terms, the right of an employee to all or part of the employer's contributions, whether in the form of cash or as a deferred pension.

Voluntary accumulation plan: A plan offered by mutual fund